T0369051

MERCY

Written By Michael J. Rodgers, Jr.

2009

Order this book online at www.trafford.com
or email orders@trafford.com

Most Trafford titles are also available at major online book retailers.

Printed in Victoria, BC, Canada.

ISBN: 978-1-4269-2507-8 (sc)

*Our mission is to efficiently provide the world's finest, most comprehensive book publishing
service, enabling every author to experience success. To find out how to publish your book, your
way, and have it available worldwide, visit us online at www.trafford.com*

Trafford rev. 1/13/2010

 www.trafford.com

North America & international
toll-free: 1 888 232 4444 (USA & Canada)
phone: 250 383 6864 ♦ fax: 812 355 4082

DEDICATION

To my wife and kids, without you nothing would be possible.

CONTENTS

Acknowlegdement

I would like to thank God for all the blessings he has given me and my family. I also want to thank my wife who has stood by me through all my struggles, while I worked on the road and the decisions I made along the way, as well as the decision to join the United States Army. I also want to thank my two awesome kids who I love so very much. I want to thank Pastor Jim Young and Pastor Tim Fall who have been there for me and my family. I would also like to thank my church family and friends who have always been there with blessings and love. I want to thank all the soldiers who have and are fighting for our freedom, to those that have given the ultimate sacrifice and to those families that struggle each day without the one they love due to the wars and other violence that exist throughout the world.

CHAPTER I

On April 2, 2005, I gave my life to the Lord and was born again. On that day I felt a presence and a power come over me that I could never truly explain. That presence and power began to help me with my present and future situations and deal with the past that I continuously tried to push away but continued to come up and affect my present life in many ways. I struggled in many aspects of my life from relationships to family and love. Over the span of my lifetime, I messed up a whole lot and hurt many people who cared about me. Even though I was screwed up in so many ways, the Lord Jesus Christ accepted me for who I was and began to work on me and my struggles. There were many times when I wanted to tuck and run back to my old life of alcohol, anger, lust, misery, pain, and self-indulgence. In these times that I struggled and fought with my inner demons, the Lord held my hand and stuck by me even through my toughest times.

This is where my story begins. I was born in December of 1979 in a small town in central Michigan. My family had moved there from the slums of Detroit. Life in Detroit was tough and dangerous and both my parents grew up on the streets and knew all about drugs, violence and poverty. Just before I was born, they decided to move to a better environment to raise a family in a smaller community with less crime and drugs. My father chose to take a job with a new construction firm and my mom was to stay home and raise me. Everything seemed to be going well for my parents. We had a nice house in the country with plenty of friends and nice cars — everything my parents could have dreamed of; everything an American family dreams of, especially a family from the slums of Detroit. I rarely heard my parents fight and they seemed happy and in love most of the time. My father would usually be home by dark and my mom would have supper and the table set when he got home. In 1981, my brother, Tommy, was born and in 1985, my sister, Rebecca, was born. My mother had a tough time with my sister's pregnancy and being able to take care of our needs once she was born. She was also taking a lot of medicine and sleeping a lot. My father, on the other hand, also changed but instead of looking at my sister with disgust, it was my mom and me who seemed to be thorns in his side. I was also going to start school in the fall and was very excited and looking forward to meeting new kids and learning. That summer everything began to change and that would begin to mold my future and the future of my family. I didn't think things would get worse with my family beyond the hatred that was already building between my father and mom but this was only the beginning. My father's luck continued to get worse and his hate for me began to grow even more. I became the focus point of his anger and his outlet. My father's job closed its doors because of economic concerns and more opportunities in another state where business was expanding and the owner wanted to concentrate his efforts there. My father was able to find another construction job right away but for much less money and a rougher group of friends who liked to drink and party. My father had to work more, things began to get tougher financially and bills began to get tougher to pay. We also got a new neighbor that moved next door to us. She and my mom hit it off right away and became best of friends. It gave my mom someone to talk to and they had a lot in common. She was from the Detroit area just like my parents and she seemed to make my mother happy when she was around. Everything seemed to be going alright for the next couple of months. Things had definitely changed but we were all adapting. My father was gone a lot working extra hours due to the pay cut and partying. My mother was still at home and was trying to do her usual duties but most of the time they would fall on me or not get done. Sheila, the next-door neighbor, was there most of the afternoon while my father worked. Sheila and my mom spent most of their time locked in the bedroom in which we were not allowed to go. We would see one or the other when my sister needed a diaper change, which was usually overdue and she was crying. When we got hungry I would fix us something to eat. I had watched my mom fix my sister's bottles and even though I wasn't sure what I was doing, I would fix my sister a bottle and then I would try to burp her. I couldn't reach the stove and was afraid I would burn myself so I wouldn't use it. So when my brother and I got hungry, I would grab a chair and get the peanut butter and bread to make us sandwiches. Every night before my father got home, Sheila and my mom would walk out of the bedroom. My mom usually didn't say a word or look at any of us. Sheila would order us to our rooms and would put Rebecca in her crib. I would hear the screen door shut and Sheila would be gone. Every night she managed to get everything done before my father walked in the door. For the rest of the night, things would seem to be fine but every night we could hear them yelling and fighting about money, the house, us kids and work. From time to time, we would also hear loud noises like things breaking and my mom crying. My mom would always say that she fell and landed on this or that. My father began to stay at work longer and most of the time we wouldn't see my father at supper time anymore. We would be awakened early in the mornings by my parents fighting and I would hear my mom yelling at him because he was drunk. This was the beginning of how our lives changed from getting away from the violence, drugs and crime to living with these things in our lives every day plus more.

A few months passed and things were still going bad and about to get worse. Sheila and my mother were in the bedroom when my mom called for me. This usually meant they wanted something from the kitchen or wanted me to check on the other kids. My brother and sister had both just fallen asleep so I knew that wasn't what they wanted. Both of them would be sleeping for the next couple of hours. I will never forget this day and still remember what I was watching on television: Thunder Cats. As I got to the door, Sheila opened it with a smile and told me to go in. At the time I had no idea what was going on. I had never entered my mom's room when Sheila had been there. As I entered the room, my mom lay naked on the bed with her eyes barely open. On the lamp stand were all kinds of things and at the time I had no idea what most of it was. I realize now it was everything needed to do crack including needles, lighter, spoons and tie-offs. I had plenty of emotions flowing through me. I was embarrassed, scared and confused about what was going on. My mom was acting all weird and wasn't moving very fast. Sheila grabbed my hand and led me over to the bed where she began to rub her hand up and down my mom's leg. She then proceeded to touch her between her legs and mom began to move a lot. As I was watching Sheila with my mom, she began to talk to me telling me about what she was doing.

"A woman needs to be taken care of and she has a lot of needs. Do you understand, Sammy?" Sheila said.

"Yes," I replied.

"Your father is not taking care of your mom. So this means you are the next person in line to take care of her needs," Sheila said.

"Ok," I replied, unsure of what that meant.

"It will be your job to make your mom and me feel good and take care of our needs. Do you understand?"

"Yes," I said a little scared and with a tear coming down my eye, which she wiped away.

At this time it seemed as if my mom was sleeping. Her eyes were closed and she wasn't moving. A few minutes passed. Sheila then turned around and had me help her undress. I still remember every detail and everything running through my mind, even what Sheila smelled like. I was terrified and wanted it to stop but it continued and I did what I was told. She was wearing a white tank top and jeans. She had me first take of her tank top, which exposed a lacy black bra. I struggled to unsnap her bra so she helped. This made her breast fall out and they were at my eye level and I was amazed and shocked at the same time. She gave me a smile then proceeded to take off her pants. She took a few steps back, standing there only in her black panties.

"What do you think?" she asked.

"I don't know," I said, not knowing what to say or do. Looking back, she had nearly a perfect body but I didn't know what to say.

She began to walk back to me and began to touch and rub herself through her panties. After a few minutes, she moved down kissing me on my lips and then stuck her tongue in my mouth. After awhile, she pulled up a chair and told me to just watch and enjoy.

"One day you will please us both, Sammy. You are a great student and you better believe I am going to continue to teach you."

She turned around and began to focus all her attention on my mom. She began to rub, lick, suck my mom's body parts until she began to moan and yell. They both began to kiss and then Sheila rolled over lying on her back. As they both lay there beside one another, Sheila looked at me.

"Come lay with us, Sammy. It's alright, you did a good job and you will continue to learn and get better so that one day you can do the same for us both. Hop into bed between the two of us," she said.

As I lay between Sheila and Mom. They both put their naked thighs on mine. They both look down at me and gave me a kiss on my forehead. I wanted to cry. I didn't understand what was going on. I just continued to lay there until it was time for Sheila to leave. This was the first of many days to come when I lay between Sheila and my mom.

Shortly after leaving the room, I heard Rebecca crying. I went to her and got her out of the crib. I took her to the living room where I lay her down with her toys. As I made the bottle, I noticed Sheila was changing Rebecca's diaper before she left. My mom was still not up and I figured she probably wouldn't be up for a while. Sheila left and I turned on the television where I began to watch some cartoons. I sat there confused, scared and sad, and began to cry over the current events. I wasn't sure of what just happened or even why I was crying but I certainly didn't feel good. After awhile, I just stopped thinking about it and began to take care of Rebecca and Tommy, who finally woke up. Every once in awhile, I would envision Sheila and what she said before she left.

"See you tomorrow," she said with a huge smile. She gave me another kiss on the lips and began to walk away.

She turned around again and said, "Your mom will be out in a bit. Just be quiet and leave her alone, Sam."

"Ok," I replied and she left.

I sat there continuing to think about Sheila. I was hoping that tomorrow would never come and I would never see Sheila again. A couple of hours passed and Mom had not made it out of the bedroom. It was getting dark outside, which usually meant my father would be coming home. Tommy and I were getting really hungry and Rebecca had a full diaper. I figured I better go check on my mom. As I got to the bedroom door, I saw headlights pull into the driveway. I hurried and opened the door and saw my mom still lying naked on the bed with a sheet covering half her body. She looked up at me half-dazed. "Father just pulled into the driveway, Mom." Then she must have realized what I said because she hurried to her feet. She was stumbling trying to find some clothes and clean up the mess on the nightstand. I told her that Rebecca had a full diaper also and she just gave me a glare like she had too many worries to think about and that was not what she wanted to hear. She must have decided that the diaper needed to be changed first because she headed straight to Rebecca to change her diaper. Before she could get done changing Rebecca, my father came through the door. I hurried to my father, hoping to feel a little hope and love. Instead, as I got to him, he handed me his lunch pail and told me to take care of it. As I turned to do as he said, he called me back. I turned to see him looking at the dishes and the mess in the kitchen. He turned to me, grabbing me by the face with his hand.

"You are worthless, just like your mother. Worthless, worthless, worthless! You will be nothing, just like her. Now go take care of that."

I noticed he was heading straight to the living room where my mom was. I hurried and took care of the lunch pail and ran back. As I was almost to the living room, I heard my father yelling at my mom. He was calling her lazy, worthless and a whore. She began to cry and began yelling back at him calling him a drunk and a bastard. As I entered the living room, I saw my father take a step forward and hit my mom with the back of his hand. She stumbled backwards, tripping over Rebecca and falling to the floor. She looked up at him wiping the blood from her mouth.

"I'm sorry," Mom said.

"I know you are," father said.

Rebecca and Tommy were both crying. My mom began to get up when my father started toward her again. I ran and grabbed a hold of my father's leg, trying to stop him from getting to my mom. He reached down grabbing me by my hair and threw me on the couch. He grabbed a hold of my mom by the arm and pulled her to her feet.

"Get the hell in the kitchen and fix something to eat," Father said.

"Screw you," she said. He reached back to hit her again.

"Stop, Father!" I said.

My mom looked at me with tears in her eyes and got up and headed to the kitchen. He then fixed his eyes on me. He told me to come to him. As I went I was slow and uncertain what was going to happen next. I had never seen my father quite like this or even seen my parents fight right in front of me. As I got a few feet from him he told me to bend over the coffee table. I wasn't sure what was going to happen but I was sure it wasn't good. I had never been spanked before. I looked over my shoulder and noticed my father taking off his belt. I began to cry and was hoping it wouldn't hurt.

"Never get in the way again, do you hear me, Sam!"

"Yes, Father."

"If you do it again it will be much worse. Do you hear me?"

"Yes, Father."

I was crying a lot harder at this point. Then suddenly his belt hit me across my butt and back of my legs. It sent a sensation of pain throughout my body. He continued to hit me with his belt several times, missing my butt completely and hitting me across my back and my legs. A couple of times the belt twisted around my side slapping me in the stomach. The whole time I was crying telling him how sorry I was. He would only respond with, "Of course you are sorry and you always will be, Sam. So, just shut up and take it."

Tommy and Rebecca were crying and Tommy ran into the kitchen to Mom. Mom sent him to the bedroom to play. When father was all done he looked down at me with disgust and then spit on me. He then went to Rebecca and picked her up smiling and playing with her like nothing had just happened and after a few moments she stopped crying. I headed into the kitchen where I saw Mom with tears in her eyes.

"Honey, will you get some corn from the storage room?" she asked.

I went and got her the corn and then went and played with Tommy. A few minutes later, I heard father say he was going to take a shower. We continued to play until Mom called us out to set the table for supper. As we were setting the table, Father came out of the bathroom. We all sat down at the table to eat. As I sat down the burning and pain hurt a little more when I finally sat down at the table. I was trying to avoid looking at my father but then he said, "Sammy, I am sorry I had to punish you. If you weren't such a terrible and worthless kid and acted more like Tommy, maybe you wouldn't need to be punished."

After we ate, my father gave my mom a kiss and went to the living room. My mom turned and told Tommy and I that we were going to take a bath. She went to the bathroom and started the bath water.

"Take off your clothes, guys," Mom said.

As I was taking off my clothes, I noticed my shirt had blood on it and it was sticking to my back. My mom helped me take it off and the pain was unbearable. She looked at me with sympathy but didn't say a word. I stepped into the tub and when I sat down the water made my back and butt sting. I began to cry because of the pain. My mom looked at me very sternly and said, "I understand it hurts, Sammy, but you need to suck it up and after a few minutes the pain will go away."

She was right, the pain did go away and we continued to get cleaned up and play. My mom went to the kitchen and continued to clean and later that night we all went to bed, but I just lay there because I could not sleep. I couldn't get the thoughts out of my head from the events of the day; I lay there crying, wondering why my parents hated me and what I did so wrong to deserve it. I could hear noises coming from my parents' room as well. I could hear them yelling and the sounds of things breaking. I was sad and angry at my father because of what he did to my mom and was also afraid for her. All I could think of was to pray. My grandmother went to church every weekend and she would talk to me from time to time and would tell me to pray when I was sad or needed something. So that is what I did.

"Lord, I am sorry for being a bad kid. I wish I could be better. Will you please show me and teach me how to be better so that my parents can be happy? Please make this all stop. It hurts and I am scared. Please help my mom; she is being hurt by my father and my father needs help too. I love them. Will you please help us? Amen."

CHAPTER 2

Now that I look back on that day, I realize that was the beginning of the hell that I would go through. I was only five years old but I can still remember it like it was yesterday. My first marriage was in 1998 with my girlfriend from high school. It was a great relationship; she didn't bother me much about drinking and drugs. Some other positive notes where that she didn't want kids and her parents hated me. The best part of our relationship was the fact that I didn't have to deal with her stuck-up parents because even if they liked me I would not care if I ever saw them. I didn't want anyone in our business. Shortly after getting married, I began to work on the road and was usually gone for several months at a time. I enjoyed working on the road it gave me the freedom to do what I wanted with no regrets or someone telling me I couldn't do something. At the same time, I had someone waiting for me back home. I didn't want the responsibility that came with being a husband and definitely didn't want someone trying to control things. I also did not want any kids and I made that very clear to her. I always told myself it was because I was selfish and wanted too many things in life to have kids. The truth was that I didn't want to have the things that happened to me to happen to them. My job was to conduct surveys, corrosion testing to pipelines across the United States. I enjoyed the work and the lifestyle. We would play as hard as we worked. We worked for the weekends. When it came to the weekend, I was drunk from Friday night until Sunday night. When Friday's shift was over, we would pull into the local liquor store and get the night started. Usually I would grab a bottle of Jose Cuervo and some Bud Light. My weekend consisted of liquor, women and fighting, and a weekend was not complete if I didn't do one of these steps. There wasn't a weekend when I didn't take a girl back to the hotel and get into a fight. One particular night we went over to a bar across from our hotel. We always tried to keep a bar as close as possible to wherever we stayed. I had slammed a couple of shots of tequila and a couple of beers before meeting up and going over with the rest of the crew. It was a rather large bar and at this point not too many people were there but it was still pretty early in the evening. I walked to the bar and bought a round for me and my buddies. We sat at the bar a while and at about ten o'clock the place started to get busy and the women were filing in. There were a lot of beautiful women but this night it wouldn't have really mattered. This night one particular woman caught my eye. She was a beautiful brunette who sat over in the corner of the bar with a couple of other women and two other guys. I watched her for a while making sure she wasn't with either of the two guys, which really didn't matter much to me. As I watched her on the dance floor, I had to have her; she was so sexy and the way she moved made her even sexier. At midnight I went over and asked her to dance. At first she said no then she looked around, got up and we headed to the dance floor. Out on the dance floor it was hot and we must have stayed out there for three songs until a slow song began to play. We continued to dance and I began to tell her that I wanted her; I even told her what I wanted to do to her. She gave me a playful slap and a smile. After the song we both headed back to our seats. After a few drinks I had a drink sent her way. I waited a few minutes then headed over to her table. As I got over to the table, one of the guys stood up. I advised him to take his seat and made a joke that there was no need for him to stand at attention for me. He gave me a look and took his seat when his wife tugged at his shirt. I looked at Crystal and told her I was leaving and that I wanted her to join me back at my hotel. At first she hesitated and the guy who stood up before opened his mouth.

"She's not leaving with anyone except us and even if she was to leave with anyone else it wouldn't be you," he said.

"Yes, I believe I am ready to go," Crystal said.

"What are you doing?" he asked.

Then he grabbed her arm. She looked him in the eyes with a look that could kill and then pulled away.

"I will see you all tomorrow," Crystal said, giving one of the other females a smile.

The guy gave me a glare of hate as I walked away. I loved it and gave him a smile in return. Once over to the hotel room she was all over me. I had a hard time even getting the door open. She had my pants undone before the door even closed. As we entered the room, I scooped her up, slamming her against the wall as we began to go into a heavy and heated kissing frenzy. I ripped off her shirt with her buttons going in all directions, exposing her black laced bra. I then proceeded to ride her black skirt up and tore off her panties. We proceeded down the hall with her legs wrapped around my waist until we made it to the bed where I dropped her. She got on her knees and began crawling to me. Once at the edge of the bed, she grabbed my belt and pulled down my pants, letting them drop to the floor. She then ran her hands up my abs, pulling my shirt over my head. Then she began to kiss me, starting from my neck and going to my groan. The rest of the night was a fast thrill ride. The last time I saw the clock it was four-thirty. We finally fell asleep and I was exhausted; it was more like my body gave in. The next morning I awoke with my back stinging and not remembering from what. I looked in the mirror and noticed my back was all scratched up. As I walked out of the bathroom she was waking up. She got up giving me a kiss. She grabbed my hand and led me to the shower where we began where we left off the night before. After awhile, she left and I headed to lunch with the guys. That night I went back to the same bar and like the night before, it was dead until about ten o'clock. At about ten-thirty, Crystal's group arrived but she was not with them but there was an additional two guys with them. I knew there would be trouble and I was actually looking forward to it. I told my buddy Jake what was up and he just gave me a smile so I knew he was up for a little fun. As the night went on, I noticed them eyeing me and getting a little antsy. One of them must have drank enough courage and decided to come over to our table. He had a drink in his hand and decided to pour it directly over my head as he was walking by acting as if he tripped and that it was an accident. I stood up quickly but kept my cool, realizing there would be four of them eventually. The guy who poured the drink over my head was definitely in my target but he wasn't going to be the first to fall. There was one that was making his way over that was much bigger and looked like he knew how to fight just by the way he carried himself. So I hit the first guy who poured the drink and as he stumbled backwards I went after the one coming. Jake also stood up noticing another one coming and swung his beer bottle slamming it against his head. He dropped to the floor and was out cold. I was after the big guy barreling toward me. He had a limp to his right side and knowing he wouldn't be able to maneuver quickly to that side I stepped to my left and let him pass. I turned around to meet him and as he turned I put my right foot to the top of his knee buckling it and dropping him to the floor in pain. While still on one knee looking up at me, I gave him one good hit to the side of his face, making his face flatten out. I then gave him a kick to the side of his head. His eyes rolled and he fell backward and was out cold. I then looked over my shoulder just in time to see a fist flying toward my head. I turned and blocked it with my forearm. As I blocked the punch, he dropped his left hand, leaving his head wide open. So I hit him with a right jab to the nose. Jake was also in a good fight behind us. The guy I was fighting grabbed at his nose, which was bleeding everywhere. I came forward with another right jab and then a left hook, sending him to the floor. I followed him to the floor, pinning his arms with my knees and began to hit him several times until I heard Jake yell for help. I got up and headed a few feet from me where I grabbed the guy, spinning him around and landing a right to his jaw. He spun around where Jake was waiting and nailed him again. I grabbed hold of him in a full nelson, letting Jake continue to pound on him. When I felt his knees get weak, I let him go. He just dropped like a sack of clothes. We finished our shots real quick and left before the cops showed up. This was a typical weekend for us. I enjoyed the freedom and the feeling of working, drinking and the fighting. It all gave me a release from reality. I felt like I could do what I wanted and no one would stop me, and if they tried I didn't need them. Another incident that happened on that trip was about a month later in Clanton, Al., we had been there only a few days and the job was giving us fits. The equipment and weather was working against us and it seemed like support was a light year away. It was Friday night and my boss and I had just had an argument about the job and the equipment that was sent out with me. Someone at the office had failed to mention that certain equipment would be mailed to the site, but this equipment was needed to kick off the job and it was going to be a week late, setting us back and making our jobs more difficult. At the end of our conversation, we both came to an agreement and were content with how to proceed. I was still feeling a little tense and it was Friday night. I stopped by the liquor store, which was right next to our hotel, and picked up a bottle of tequila and lime. I continued back to the hotel and began sipping on the tequila and then continued to do shots. I always kept salt with me and a knife to slice the lime. I continued drinking as I was completing my tasks for the night. By the time I took a shower, sent my emails and got dressed for the night out, the fifth was gone. I didn't realize the time and how fast I drank the bottle; when I looked at the clock only an hour had passed since I began. We were going to meet in room 148 where my assistant was staying before we all headed out for the evening. As I got to his room, I could feel the tequila catching up with me and as I got into the room, I flopped on the love seat just inside the door. The guys knew I had already started and threw a few jokes. Then Rob threw me a Bud Light and I began to drink away on that. After a couple of beers, we headed across the street to a bar named Charlie Brown's. Once we got in, we order a couple rounds of drinks and headed to the pool tables. I was alright at pool, no expert but I enjoyed playing. I started off shooting great and was having a great time. Somewhere along the way, the tequila snuck up on me. Supposedly, the bar ran out of cigarettes so I ran — stumbled — across the street to get some. At this point I do not remember a thing. The next thing I remembered was the sun shining in my face and looking up at a dozen other guys. I lifted up my head, looking around and asked where I was. They said I was in the county lock up and that I had been there since around two-thirty in the morning. My head was spinning and I was covered in puke. I closed my eyes and fell back asleep on the 2x6 bench that I had been lying on. A short while later, they woke me for breakfast. It smelled as bad as it looked and tasted even worse. I had slimy snotty eggs, overcooked bacon and two pieces of burnt toast. The officer delivering the breakfast looked at me and just shook his head in amazement. I looked at him and asked what had happened.

"You don't remember," the officer asked.

"No, I don't, sir."

"The officers on duty told me you started at the liquor store and then all hell broke loose."

"What do you mean?"

Well he proceeded to tell me that at the liquor store they couldn't understand what I wanted and I got upset and cursed my way out. Then I stumbled across the parking lot until I reached the six-lane road that separated me from the bar. An eighteen-wheeler had been watching me and slowed down, realizing that I was drunk and heading for road. Once I got to the road, I tripped over the curb and lay in the middle of the lane. The semi blocked the toad until the officers arrived. The officers had a hard time getting me in the car but eventually got me here. I asked when I could leave and if I could make a call. He said I would need to show up for court and that I would need to get bonded out. I finally got hold of my assistant foreman and a bail bondsman who would bond me. Since I was from out of state, it took me several tries but eventually I got out. For the next two days I was hung-over and my weekend was shot. Once my date arrived they charged me with public intoxication, public disorderly and made me pay $375.00 in fines and court fees. I stayed out for about another two months. On my way home, I got a message that I was to head to California the following day since my job lasted longer and the other job had to start on this day. There was no time to stay at home. So after one night at home, I hit the road again, this time flying to Los Angeles where I would be met by Andy Tobin who was the project engineer for the west coast office.

CHAPTER 3

The next morning when I woke I could smell the breakfast Mom was fixing. I was starving and my belly was growling. I made it to the kitchen and Mom was standing at the stove flipping bacon and turning the sausage links. She would cook every Saturday. Now, remembering that it was Saturday, I realized Sheila wouldn't be over. She must have either meant that she would see me on Monday or she just forgot that today was Saturday; either way, it didn't matter. I would see her on Monday. Mom called us all to the table where it was already set and all the fixings were already out. As we were sitting down, my mom brought over the bacon and sausage and sat it on the table. I looked up at my mom and noticed both of her eyes were black and she had a cut on her lip. I didn't say anything to my mom but knew that my father had hit her again. When we finished eating, I gave my mom a kiss and a hug and thanked her for the breakfast. Every Saturday

I had to work out in the yard no matter what time of the year. Most of the time my job was stacking wood that my father would be cutting and splitting. My father would cut and split and I just had to keep moving the wood out of his way and stacking it. What didn't get done on the weekend I had to stack during the week. He would always say if you want to keep warm and if you want me to continue to feed you then you will work. I was only five years old but he didn't care; if I gave any sign of quitting he would go on and yell for twenty minutes, sometimes hitting and kicking me. So most of the time I kept my mouth shut and just tried to keep up. We would start right after breakfast and stop just before dark. We would take a break at lunch and whenever the chainsaw needed gas and oil. My father always had a bottle of Jack Daniels sitting nearby that he would sip on from time to time. This was a typical weekend when my father was around on Saturday and Sunday. Usually by the end of the night, father was buzzed and would yell some, eat supper and fall asleep in the recliner watching television. I was always glad when the weekend was over. This meant school and that my father would be at work. This also meant that Sheila would be over and I was still scared and feeling weird inside about what happened on Friday. My back and body was still sore on my way to school Monday. My back still hurt from the belt and from all the work we did that weekend. I think we may have stacked more wood that weekend than we had any previous weekends, and at times I struggled to carry the pieces my father would cut. I enjoyed going to school; it gave me a break from home and I loved learning. My favorite subject was math and I prided myself in knowing more than the other kids when it came to the subject. As if nothing else could have gone wrong, I got into a fight that day. We were all out on the playground when a kid named Tony called my mom a bitch! My anger exploded and I tackled the kid and began to punch him in the face. The playground teacher ran over and pulled me off him. I gave him a bloody nose and a fat lip. I was sent to the principal's office. I sat down in the chair near the office until the principal arrived. After a lecture I was sent back to my classroom and didn't get into any trouble. The rest of the day my friends thought I was the coolest. Once school was over, I hurried to the bus and hopped into the first seat right behind the bus driver. All the way home I thought about the weekend, the fight and then about Sheila. Boy, I hoped she wasn't at the house. I finally arrived home and ran off the bus to the house. I quickly opened the door, throwing my coat by the door and kicking my boots off. As I got into the living room, I noticed Sheila sitting on the couch watching some soap opera that was on television.

"Your brother and sister are taking a nap so be as a quiet as possible, alright," she said.

She asked me how school was and I told her everything. She gave me a smile about the fight telling me good job for sticking up for my mom but not to make a habit of it. She then told me my mom wasn't feeling well. She then looked up at me and told me to come sit next to her. My stomach began to hurt as I slowly made my way to the couch. Once over there, she started talking to me about Friday and how good I did. After a few minutes, she began to get undressed. Once she was totally undressed, except her underwear, she leaned over, giving me a kiss and then grabbing hold of my hand. She ran my hand down her body until I reached her underwear where she made me rub her until she told me to stop. Then she made me sit on the floor and watch her do the same to herself. She took off her underwear and began pleasing herself. For the next half hour, I sat there with my mind racing about what I was seeing and how Sheila looked. She then got up and went to the bathroom. Several minutes later, she returned, giving me kiss on my lips and sticking her tongue in my mouth again for about a minute, and then began to get dressed. After she was dressed, she went to my mom's room where she stayed for the next hour. Over the next hour, I sat on the couch watching cartoons but the only thing I kept seeing was Sheila and her naked body. My emotions were going crazy and I didn't know if I was right or wrong. Was this normal? I guess it was and I must adapt and learn to deal with it and that is what I eventually would do. Sheila would continue to come over every day of the week. Most of the time I would experience this sexual experience with only Sheila, but from time to time she would include Mom. Most of the time Mom was all drugged up. I also had to deal with Father. He was drinking more and more. The only good thing was that usually I didn't see him until the weekend since he didn't return home until after I was in bed during the week. The weekends consisted of working on wood or whatever else Father could come up with. It also wasn't unusual to see Mom and Father fighting and arguing, and from time to time things breaking or Mom getting hurt. The one thing that was changing was that our workdays were getting shorter on the weekends. Father was usually drunk by the mid-afternoon, which usually meant we stopped working or at least he did. Catching a backhand, belt or anything else my father could grab continued but now more frequently. It typically happened every weekend. During one incident, he even broke my arm. We were out doing wood when I tossed a piece and it hit him in the foot. So he grabbed a piece of wood and slammed it against my arm, breaking my arm in two places. When I screamed in pain, I received a backhand and was told to shut up and get tougher. After a few minutes, he most have realized that my arm was broken and what he had just done because he grabbed me by the shoulders and told me I fell out of a tree. That is what he told me I had to tell the doctors once we got to the hospital. On the way to the hospital, he reminded me of this and told me that I would be taken away from my Mom and from my brother and sister if I told them the truth. When I got to the hospital, I did as I was told. The doctor and nurses kept asking me what happened. At one point I even saw my father and the doctor arguing. After a couple of hours, I left the hospital with a cast on and some medicine. Over the next few years, things continued to stay the same but also continued to get worse. My father was drunk most of the time and he was always angry. My mom, well she was doing more and more drugs and it seemed as if she never came out of the bedroom, which meant more work for me to do. As my brother and sister got older, they would help me but I tried to take most of the work myself so they wouldn't have to. This helped to keep Mom out of trouble, at least some of it, which meant less fighting. Sheila was the only one I felt cared or at least gave me some hope and happiness. She continued to come over every day and her expectations and wants continued to increase but at least she made me feel good and told me she loved me. I began to enjoy Mondays and knowing that the weekend was over and that I would see Sheila. This lifestyle and everyday grind continued for the most part, not changing much until the summer of 1991 when things began to change a little. I was entering the sixth grade and my anger began to catch up with me. My father also began to drive a truck that summer and was gone most of the time. He would come home every other weekend, usually depending on work. This year would be the next turning point of my life.

CHAPTER 4

I had been gone now about three months working in Arizona for El Paso Natural Gas Company and in California for the city of San Ramon. These were typical jobs but in this case the expectations were a lot higher. There had been some concern for safety on the gas lines so the D.O.T. was breathing down their necks to get results, which everything rolls downhill so we were feeling the pressure too. The companies we were working for were doing their jobs and taking all the right precautions but there were still concerns like there should be in any sensitive situation. In the end all turned out well, making the client and my company happy. The data and job performance allowed us to secure us more jobs for future dates and a nice bonus. We drove the entire way back from Flagstaff, AZ, to Michigan non-stop. I got back to the shop and had my buddy drive me home since I left my truck at home before I demobbed. I walked in the house; it was empty and all my phones calls to everyone including Stacy were not being answered. So I flopped on the couch and flipped on the television to ESPN. I sat there catching up on what I had missed from the day before since I was driving home and missed all the games. I must have dosed off because the next thing I remembered was being shaken to wake up. It was my wife and her sister. They were bringing in some food and were very surprised to see me. My wife jumped on my lap and began giving me kisses. We both got up and I helped take care of things. Her sister left after a few minutes and we headed straight to the bedroom where we stayed for the next couple of hours. She was glad to see me and excited to have me home for some fun. Afterward, we both got into the shower and then got into our bar clothes for a night on the town. We called a few friends to get everyone together and meet at a small local bar to get started. By nine o'clock there were about ten of us and a bunch of other locals having a few beers and shooting some pool. After a bit we all decided to head to another bar a few towns away where there is a dance floor and better music. Once we got there my buddies bought a round of Yeager bombs for all the guys and the night began with a bang. That first round went down real good and my buddies kept them coming. My wife and Jessica, my wife's best friend, were out on the dance floor having a good time and looking very sexy. On the way back to the table, a guy grabbed my wife by the arm and asked her to dance. She told him "no" and tried to walk away but he kept asking even when she said she was married. I had a reputation for fighting and many of the people knew me at the bar, but this guy I had never seen before. I saw what was happening from across the room and I got up and headed over, trying to keep my cool. The bouncer who was also a friend gave me a look like don't do anything stupid. As a got closer to the situation, I saw a few people back away and one guy give another a nudge. They knew what was about to go down even though I was going to try to end the night without any troubles. Once I made my way over, I asked if there was a problem.

"No problem at all," he said, "I was just hoping to dance with this sexy woman who keeps shutting me down."

"She's married to me and that would be a NO!"

"That's too bad. She deserves better than a smuck like you."

I considered that to be an invitation to fight and so did those around the bar that heard it because I heard a lot of mumbling in the background. I slowly moved my wife out of the way. She also knew what was going to happen and she hated it when I fought. She looked terrified, which didn't really affect me too much because in the end it would be alright. Then I nailed the guy straight in the throat, causing him to gasp for air and fall back, taking a seat on the pool table. Then I grabbed him by the shirt and looked him in the eyes and told him, "If I ever see you again I won't be so nice and your family will be preparing funeral arrangements." I threw him backward and told him to leave. Once he got his breath, he got up and him and a couple of his buddies left the bar. The rest of the night went well except that one of my buddies puked in the back seat of my car on the way home. It stunk up the entire car for the rest of the ride home; luckily my seats were made of leather so it should be a little easier to get cleaned in the morning. Fortunately, my wife didn't drink much that night and was able to drive us home because we were too drunk to stand let alone drive. The next day I woke up looking down at my wife who had fallen off the bed. She said I pushed her off the bed when I was tossing and turning. *Yeah right*, I thought. I knew she fell off on her own but either way it was quite funny. My head was pounding, the light was killing my eyes and I needed Mt. Dew or a beer, whichever we had to help with the hangover. I stumbled a bit when I got up and headed to the refrigerator where the first thing I saw was a beer. I cracked it open and felt better as soon as the first drink went down my throat. Stacy got up and cooked up some breakfast. We had omelets, toast and some orange juice. There is nothing better than a good breakfast after a good drunk. It tasted so good; it hit the spot and helped with the hangover. The breakfast reenergized me and made my hangover go away for the most part so I grabbed another beer. I was only scheduled home for a week so my wife had big plans all week when all I wanted to do was relax and party. The first thing though that she had to do was go with her mother for some grocery shopping to get things for her grandmother, who was not able to get out of the house anymore due to cancer. They would be away awhile so I took a shower and then started to watch a movie. Just as the movie started to get good, the doorbell rang. I got up and answered the door; it was Stacy's sister.

"Is Stacy home?" she asked, knowing that she wasn't.

"No."

"Good, there is something I want to tell you."

"Come on in then."

Once she got inside, she took off her coat and was wearing a sexy blouse that exposed most of her breasts.

"You know I have always been attracted to you and that it was me you truly wanted back in school, not my sister," she said all cocky and sexy.

"That's true but I took the sister that was willing at the time," I replied.

"Well I'm willing now."

"What about your sister?"

"What she doesn't know won't hurt her."

I really didn't care either way. I didn't truly love Stacy or any woman in fact. So, I figured why not. If she doesn't say anything all the better and WOW was she sexy! She must have been waiting for this moment for a long time because she didn't hesitate one bit. For the next hour, I let Lisa abuse my body and I enjoyed every moment. We had sex in the kitchen and living room in and out of position as if I was starring in a porno. We did stay away from the bedroom. It may have been the best sex that I had up to that moment. Afterward, we both lay on the floor with smiles on our faces, talking about how great it was and coming up with ideas of when we would get together next. The rest of the week was ridiculous but a lot of fun trying to juggle both women, partying and trying not to get caught, which was the least of my worries but also added to the fun. Lisa seemed to know when and where her sister was going to be because whenever Stacy took off for a while Lisa was there with bells and whistles on. A couple of days before I was to leave was my birthday and that day was crazy and a blast. Stacy left that morning rather early to go to work and wouldn't be home until late and we were to go out for dinner and then hit the bars. I was lying there in bed tossing and turning not wanting to get up and not realizing how much time had passed. Then I heard the door shut so I thought it was Stacy thinking that it was still early and that she had just got up when in fact it had been almost an hour since she left. I figured she was returning because she had forgotten something for work. A couple of seconds later, I looked up and saw Lisa standing in the doorway.

"I figured you shouldn't be left alone on your birthday."

"Yeah, you got a present for me?"

"I certainly do."

She gave me a smile and dropped the trench coat she was wearing and she stood in the doorway in her birthday suit. Looking at her naked body and all those curves, I was wide awake. The rest of the morning we lay in bed and I was receiving one of my best birthday presents ever. After awhile we both got up, took showers and then she began to cook some lunch and gave me a beer that she brought with her, and for desert we had my favorite: chocolate-covered strawberries. She left a few hours later and luckily she did because we had a very close call. Lisa left and I hopped in the shower. A few moments later, I was joined in the shower by a woman, who I thought was Lisa returning for a second run. I was rinsing my hair and couldn't see who it was. I almost called out Lisa's name but before I did, I opened my eyes first and it was Stacy. Looking at her in surprise, I smiled and told her I was happy to see her.

We used up all the hot water getting one of my birthday presents from her early and then we headed to the bed where I was exhausted and did not think I could continue anymore. She had gotten off work early to spend some more time with me before we went out. The rest of the afternoon we lay in bed until it was time to head out to dinner where we were to meet up with some friends and Lisa. The rest of night went good; there was a lot of alcohol, marijuana and sex happening all around us. It was quite entertaining and a very good time. Out on the dance floor the ladies were rocking the joint. The night ended with a kiss from Lisa and a whisper of future promises, and Stacy and I headed back to the house loaded. The week ended up going by way too fast and I was saying goodbye to both women and heading out on the road for some hard work and fun out in Texas. Our first place we had to cover was Amarillo, TX. It took a couple of days to get there and then we had meetings and scouting to do to get the job started. So we didn't get much work done the first couple of days there but we were able to find some bars and strip clubs to pass the time. The next couple of weeks were going as always. Twelve-hour days followed by a few drinks during the week and the wild and crazy weekends. Well after about three weeks, I received a call from Stacy. She said she had good news. What could she be so excited about? It made me a little worried. Then she told me that she was pregnant. Immediately, I was angry and started getting an upset stomach. She knew I didn't want any kids and would not ever have kids. She promised me she could not have a kid, which was one reason I married her. Why would she try to play me like that? I proceeded to tell her how she tricked me and that I wasn't going to be a father. Then I told her we were done and we were getting a divorce. I told her I would get my stuff once I got home in a couple of weeks since I would be coming home early for an extended break for Christmas. She was very upset and didn't believe what I was saying and thought we could discuss it once I got home. I told her we would discuss it then and figure it all out. Once I got to thinking about it, I didn't want her to throw out my stuff so I was going to have to play it cool until I got home. I hung up and left it at that. I would have plenty of time once I got home. I wasn't scheduled to go out on the road again until the 6th of January and I would be home on the 18th of December so I had a lot of time to get everything.

CHAPTER 5

I was beginning a new year of school and I had my eyes set on a little blonde in my classroom named Lisa. I would watch her every day wishing that she would be my girlfriend. One day I came to school all excited and determined to talk to her. I had been practicing what I was going to say. I walked over to her a little nervous but confident.

"Hello, how are doing today, Lisa?"

"Good, Sam." She tried to ignore me and turned away.

"I want you to know you are beautiful and I want you to be my girl."

"Yuk, get away from me, Sam."

"Alright, Lisa, you remember that one day you will be knocking on my door."

That day I made myself believe that there wasn't a girl that was kind and that caring for a woman was meaningless because all they do is hurt you. So from that day forward I told myself never to trust or care for another girl or woman again. At home things were still crazy. Sheila came over almost every day, Mom was usually too high to realize what was going on and Father was gone most of the time driving the truck. Well the day that Lisa treated me like scum, I got off the bus and headed inside. Once inside Sheila noticed I was upset and called me over to her.

"What's the matter, Sam?" she said.

"Nothing," I replied.

She kept it up and eventually I told her about Lisa and what was said. She just looked at me and said, "I will make everything better and make you feel better."

"Ok."

"Take off your pants, Sammy."

This was the first time that Sheila had performed oral sex on me. She began to rub my penis from the outside of my underwear until I got hard. She then removed my underwear and proceeded to give me a blowjob. Every once in a while, she would stop to ask me how it felt and if I wanted her to continue. I was uncertain and excited about what was happening. I was used to and expected certain things with Sheila but this was new and it felt good, but there was always a "then what" in the back of my mind. Something always led to more and I knew that. What will I have to do to her? After that day things began to progress and I became the student again and Sheila the teacher. My brother and sister were out of harm's way as long as I did my job and that was all I thought of. It was Friday so I knew I wouldn't see Sheila until at least Monday but now I had to deal with my father. Most of the time Father would come home late Friday night or early morning and this night was no different. Around eleven o'clock I heard the door open and my father came in. He wasn't quiet and seemed to be drunk as usual. He was calling for my mom and she wasn't responding. After about five minutes, I heard my mom come out of the bedroom and ask what was wrong. I heard them talking but couldn't make out what was being said. Then I heard their bedroom door shut. I was back to sleep in minutes and not looking forward for Saturday morning. Everything was right on cue; about eight o'clock in the morning we were all being woken up to breakfast before we headed out to work. Tommy and I worked outside and Rebecca would stay in and help Mom with housework. This Saturday was a tough Saturday for Tommy; he wasn't feeling good and seemed not to do anything right. Father was starting his second bottle of whiskey and was starting to get irritated with Tommy. Tommy was stacking wood when the pile fell and almost hit him. He threw down the ax and started toward Tommy. I started toward Tommy as well.

"Father, it was my fault I told him to do it," I told him.

"Oh, is it now!"

"Yes, Father, I told him what to do and he only stacked it the way I told him to."

"You are worthless, boy."

He started toward me and I knew what would happen next. He grabbed hold of me and backhanded me, and I fell to the ground. Something at that point came over me and I got very angry and began to swing back. I was able to hit him a couple of times before he nailed me and laid me out flat. I was able to look up at him just before he kicked me in the guts, knocking the wind out of me. My mom came out the door and called everyone in just in time for lunch. My father looked at me and said, "Get up, pussy, and get inside, you got lucky this time."

"Yes, Father. I am sorry."

Then he spit on me and headed inside. After a minute or two, I got up and headed inside. My mom just looked at me with an "I am sorry" look, which I was getting used to. After lunch, Mom was able to talk my father into going shopping. This meant I was to watch the kids but also this was a way Mom could get Father out of the house and away from us. They finally left and we started watching cartoons and playing. They finally made it back later that night and brought pizza home, which was very rare for us to have. After pizza we all watched a movie together as a family, which was a good time and helped make me forget about all the stuff that had been happening. It was a rare occasion and I wished that it would always be that way, but I knew that was just stupid to actually believe. I was in some pain still from getting hit earlier but I was able to forget about some of it while watching the movie. The rest of the weekend went pretty good and there weren't any more problems, and Monday morning as usual he was on his way on the road again. Monday when I got back to school I was angry about Lisa and about my father. I wasn't going to let anyone mess with me again without fighting back and that Monday the theory was put to the test. A bully named Alex who had picked on me before started pushing me into the lockers and calling me a fag. This time though I let him have it. I felt my face get red and my anger took over. I started swinging, hitting him with my right and then the left and I continued furiously until he fell to the ground in a ball. I jumped on top of him and continued swinging, hitting him wherever I could. He began to cry and started yelling for me to stop. The other kids were crowding around yelling and cheering. Finally, a teacher grabbed hold of me and pulled me off not before I hit the teacher in the eye with one of my swinging elbows. Once the teacher got me clear of him he told me to go directly to the office. Once in the office I slammed myself into one of the seats until the principal and the teacher pulled me in the office. The teacher's eye was already swelling and it made me smile thinking about him having a black eye. They shut the door behind us and asked me what my story was. I told them what happened and of course they didn't believe me but took the story of the bully. I got detention during lunch and had to pick up trash during recess for the next two weeks. They also called my father on his cell phone and told him what happened. I felt like everyone was against me but I didn't really care anymore and this would not be my last fight. That night when I made it home, I was happy to see Sheila. At this point she was the only one who seemed to care and make me feel good. She sent the other two outside to play and we went into my bedroom. I was wondering where Mom was but most of the time she didn't come out of the bedroom when father was gone. Usually she was too drugged up to even get out of bed. The lessons continued even on this night with Sheila and this was the first night me and Sheila had sex. Afterward I felt good, I felt loved, but I also felt hate and anger toward everyone else. I didn't know what the right feelings were but I didn't care nor did it matter. It was what it was and I had to learn to adapt and survive and that is what I did. Sheila began to be the only thing on my mind. I enjoyed being with her and hated to see her go. The next thing I had to deal with was that in four days my father would be home again and I would have to deal with the consequences of my fight, but until then I was going to keep doing what I wanted to do. I continued to do all my homework and get good grades, but in the halls and during recess I was a totally different person. If someone stepped in my way or wanted to fight, I was pleased to get the practice. I got into two more fights that week alone but didn't get into any trouble for either one. One was in the locker room when one kid called me a pussy. I walked up behind him when he wasn't looking and ran his head into the locker several times and then kicked him in the guts.

"Don't fuck with me, Jason."

"Ok, Sam. Sorry."

"You better not say a word either. Do you hear me?"

He just shook his head and my reputation began as a fighter and also one not to mess with anymore. At first I thought it would mean I would have to continue to fight and I kinda liked the thought. This is how I figure I would get the respect I wanted, deserved and expected.

CHAPTER 6

I got home finally after being away for just over five weeks in which the last two I was planning where I would go once I left my wife. I thought about Lisa, but that just wouldn't work and would cause even more drama than I needed. So I called a buddy who had a pole barn and a truck. Within a couple of hours, I had all my stuff out before she got home from work. I went back to the house and waited for her to get home. When she arrived she didn't know I had taken my stuff since I didn't take any extra and my stuff really didn't make a dent in our house. I didn't need nor did I want the stuff — she could have it all. I just wanted to be done with her and the situation. She was happy to see me and gave me a kiss as she jumped on my lap. I led her into the bedroom for one last rendezvous before I broke the bad news to her. Afterward, she cooked supper and we had a couple of beers together, not saying too much, but I could tell we both were thinking about the same subject. We got done eating and I informed her I was leaving her and already had my stuff out of the house. She didn't believe me and ran to the closet to see if I was lying or not. She came out calling me every name in the book and asking me how I could do this to her.

"I told you I didn't want kids and that is what I meant. There is no gray area in the matter. I told you how I felt."

"You're such a bastard. I hate you."

"You knew the rules, Stacy, and you broke them."

"I didn't mean to. I didn't think I could get pregnant."

"Doesn't matter now, does it?"

As I turned away, I began to go to the door and she began to throw glasses and plates at me. One glass hit me in the back of the head, making a slash in my head. Blood began to flow from my head and down the back of my neck. I was ready to turn around and let her have it when I realized what my mom went through and how I said I would not ever hit a woman. So I continued out the door and out of her life. She would never call me again or ever ask for anything. I called my buddies and we decided to hit the bars and find us some women. After I got the blood to stop and I got cleaned up, we ended up just hitting some smaller bars and found no women we really wanted to take home. The next day I took all my money and started another bank account. I didn't want her hands in my money and I figured the first chance she got she would try. I filed for divorce and six months later it was granted without any disputes. I never even saw her in court. I continued to work out on the road going from one job to the next, not caring to come home; no reason to. I had what I wanted on the road: alcohol and women and nothing else really mattered to me at the time and I was making very good money not returning home. I was working in Alliance, OH, and it was a Friday night, which meant it was bar time. We ended up at a bar that had a boxing ring with barbwire for the ropes. It was rather entertaining and we were getting rowdy and drunk, having a real good time and the view was very good as well. The bar was really bringing in the ladies. The fighting ended around midnight but we were still looking for some more action. Jake and I followed a group down to the pool room and began to play pool. There were six guys and three women and two of the guys were Arabic and we had a chip on our shoulders after the 911 attacks and were still filled with hate for what happened. We began to give them looks and having a conversation that was loud enough for them to hear. They knew what was up and they were up for some action as much as we were. One of the guys decided to say something and I was ready. I walked on over to him ready for him to back down but instead he knocked my glasses off my face, breaking my brand new Oakley's. Out of my corner of my eye, I saw three bouncers coming so I backed away and figured I would continue the dance once the bar closed. The next hour I started hitting the tequila and getting into the mood. By two o'clock I was pissed and ready to destroy anything that got in my way. We walked outside and I waited for them to exit. Then I saw them come out the side door.

"Are you ready to continue what we started, pussies?"

"You got a problem with my man, fucker?" the female said.

The next thing I knew the female was running at me with the guys following and she nailed me in the nose. I chose not to hit her. I didn't like or want to hit a woman. I saw what my mom went through and I told myself I wouldn't ever hit a woman. I turned away from her and hit the first guy in my face, making him stumble backwards. Then I tackled him, slamming him to the ground and began to hit him with a right and a left while his head was bouncing off the pavement. Then I received a kick to the ribs and I rolled to the side. Once I got to the ground, I received another kick to the gut and then I was surrounded by three people including the female and began to receive one kick after another. I finally got enough energy to get up on a knee and hit one of them in the groan, sending him to the ground. Then I picked up a rock and I took a punch to the side of my head. At this point I couldn't feel a thing and I stood up, slamming the rock against his head. I saw blood fly and him drop. Out of the corner of my eye, I saw Jake fighting a guy who was three times his size but seemed to be winning the battle. I saw another guy headed my way and the female still standing beside me. Suddenly, she jumped on my back and began scratching my eyes. I grabbed hold of her wrist and twisted and threw her in front of me. She hit the ground and lay there as I slammed my foot into her chest, making her scream and gasp for air. As I turned the other guy hit me and I went down to my knee. I looked up and he hit me again, making me fall to the ground. He was a big dude and his punches made my head rattle. He jumped on top of me swinging and I put my forearms in front of my face. He got tired very quickly and I was able to work my way out and stand up before he could get up. I kicked him in the face and he fell backwards on the ground where I began to kick him in the ribs. He tried to get up again and I gave him another kick to the head and slammed the heel of my boot into his nose. Blood began to flow from his nose and lip while he lay there knocked out. The next thing I knew a van pulled up and grabbed me and Jake and said the cops were on the way and that we had to leave. Once inside the van, we realized that those inside the van were the wrestlers from inside the bar. They took us back to our hotel and dropped us off. As they left they said they would take care of things and not to worry. We both went to our beds and passed out. The next morning I woke up sore and could barely move out of bed. There wasn't a part of me that didn't hurt. I hopped into the shower to see if that would help but it didn't so I hopped back into bed. We were supposed to go to work this Saturday because we were behind but I sent the guys out without us and my assistant took over that day. When they left, Matt told me if I needed anything that his wife was in his room so just let her know. She was visiting for the weekend, which was something I allowed to happen if we were close enough to home. I was starting to get hungry so I started to get dressed when I heard a knock on the door. I answered the door and it was Matt's wife, Susan. She was holding a bag of food from McDonalds.

"You must be reading my mind. I was just getting ready to get some food."

"It was getting about lunch time so I figured you were getting a little hungry. I hope you like Quarter Pounders."

"Yes, that would be great. Thanks."

"How are you feeling?"

"I am sore but I will be alright. Thanks. It was a good night and a great fight."

As I walked back into the room, she followed behind me and shut the door. She began to ask me questions about the fight and what happened. So as I was eating I began to tell her about the night. As I got done eating, she walked over to me and ran her hand over my face where my face was swollen a bit.

"You need a woman to take care of you, Sam."

"That is true. It would be good to have a beautiful woman like you take care of me but you are married and you are married to Matt so you can't take care of my needs."

"Why? Matt is out in the field and we are all alone, so why not? He doesn't take care of my needs so I need a man to take care of mine."

"I can't argue with a woman that is in need. Can I?"

"Nope," she said with a smile.

"Now you lay there, Sam, I will do all the work. Remember I am here to take care of you."

"Ok." I wasn't going to argue.

Over the next few hours, she made me hurt and grimace in pain but it was all worth it because pleasure superseded the pain. Afterward, she lay beside me with her leg cocked up on me. We just lay there smiling looking at each other as I wondered why it didn't happen before now. I should have seen it before but must have ignored it because of Matt.

"Thank you," she said.

"You are very welcome, any time."

"Well then maybe I will see you tonight. We'll see what happens."

She got up and got dressed. Before she left she came over and gave me another kiss and said thanks again and walked out the door. Later that night, Matt and the guys returned back to the hotel. They were ready to party and I had already cracked open a beer and had a few waiting for them on ice.

"I hope my wife took care of you today, Sam," Matt said.

"Yes she did, Matt, she is a kind woman. Thanks."

"Hey anything for you, man," he said.

I had a little feeling of guilt but then it went away when I saw her walk around the corner. She was definitely out of Matt's league. After a few beers I went and got a shower and got into my bar clothes. At eight o'clock we all met outside by the trucks where we cooked out on the grill, drinking beers and tossing around the football. Every once in a while I could feel Susan's eyes on me and would turn and catch her watching me. We ran out of alcohol so Matt and Susan ran to the store to get some more and as soon as they were gone, Jake walked up to me.

"So, Sam, what happened today? How well did she take care of you?"

"She took care of me very well. She took care of all my needs."

"You lucky bastard."

"Hey, what can I say?"

"How did you know?"

"What do you mean? Her eyes are all over you and her facial expressions suggest she is thinking about more than just how great you look."

Matt and Susan returned and we continued to party out in the parking lot and in our rooms. The guys slowly started falling off and passing out. Matt was out early as usual. He was a lightweight. We always ragged on him about it but Susan was still up and partying hard. Eventually it was just Jake, Susan and me. After a while Jake gave me a look and said he was headed to bed. As soon as Jake was gone, Susan was in my arms and on my lap. That night we had sex under the stars out on the side of the hotel. She didn't want to wait to get to the room and we started right there. After a few minutes, the chair I was in collapsed and we rolled to the ground. We didn't miss a beat and continued into the wee hours of the morning. Afterward, we headed to my room, we both took showers and she disappeared again in her room. I passed out and woke up around eleven the next morning with a loud banging on my door. I opened it up it; was Jake.

"Hey, what's up? Good morning. How are you feeling?"

"I'm fine and you?"

"Not as good as you. What happened to the chair?"

"I got too drunk and passed out."

"Yeah, whatever! Matt saw her off this morning. She had a permanent smile so you must have done something right."

"Good I don't know if I could handle another night with her around."

After a few minutes of chatting about the night before, we headed out to get something to eat. The next couple of weeks went as usual. The job was going great; we were ahead of schedule by almost a week, which would probably mean at least a small bonus for each of us. One night Matt came out all excited and said he had great news. Susan was finally pregnant. He said that they had been trying for the past three years to have children and they were about to give up hope and that their relationship was suffering because of all the stress. I felt a knot develop in my stomach but I congratulated him and took all the guys out for supper to a steakhouse to celebrate. Afterward, Jake stopped by to annoy me and rub it in that I got her pregnant and that was my baby. I told him to chill and let them enjoy the moment and the life they chose. Whether the baby is mine or not, Matt will be the father. I knew this and so did Susan. She also knew I didn't want kids because Matt had told her. That weekend was going to make Matt and Susan happy because now they were going to have a child. I would not and did not want to ruin that for either of them. Susan knew what she was doing by having sex with me and even though she enjoyed it, there was a purpose to it. That was to save their marriage and have a baby they both desperately wanted. We finished the job ten days ahead of time, which meant a good bonus. I figured I was going to have a little fun once I got home. After arriving back home, I decided to stop by the local bar in Mt. Pleasant called Lucky's. As I was sitting there a beautiful brunette walked in and I was attracted to her right away. I knew I would be having a conversation with her before the night was through even if it meant letting my guard down. I didn't have a woman back home to return to and maybe it was time to find one, and this woman would make a perfect woman or wife to come home to. After a short while, I walked over to her with an extra drink in my hand. I gave her the drink and asked for permission to sit. I sat down and started talking to her and ended up talking for about two hours. She was perfect; she liked sports, drinking, playing pool and we seemed to share the same ideas. We exchanged numbers and I left feeling quite confident I would see her again. Later that night, I received a phone call that I didn't recognize but answered it anyway. It was Latisha, the woman I meant earlier at Lucky's. I hadn't programmed her number in my phone yet so I wasn't sure at first who it was. She wanted me to join her over at her place. She gave me directions and I told her I would be over in a couple of hours. I finally made it over there and she answered the door with a white teddy. I was a little shocked and amazed but I was also happy and excited to know that the events to take place were already set in motion and I didn't have to work for it. The rest of the night was sexual poetry in motion and the next morning I was awaken with the smell of breakfast and a woman cooking naked with only an apron on. I loved a woman who cooked breakfast after a long night but I especially loved a woman who did it in the nude. This couldn't get any better. At least that is what I thought at the time. This would be the first of many times we would be together. I would go on the road and actually for the first time wanted to go home to be with her. I couldn't get her off my mind and my crew could see the change. They would rag on me from time to time but it didn't bother me too much. I had enough dirt on them that I would always turn the table. I actually thought I was falling in love, which was the first time I had felt anything that even resembled what I thought was love since Sheila. Time was flying and I was enjoying my relationship and my new outlook on life. It was now 2003 and Latisha and I had been dating for about a year. I loved being around her whether we were drinking beer, watching sports or just chilling on her boat. I had not touched another woman in a year and I actually was not even tempted to want another woman. She wanted me to quit my job and come to work at a large-scale construction firm just putting in bids around the state. She hated me being gone so much and wanted to be able to get married one day, which being on the road was something that wouldn't work if I was married again. I was alright with the idea of changing jobs although I had always worked for the pipeline and knew nothing else. Her dad owned the business so she had some pull to get me the job and there was a need for another person in this position. I thought it over a bit and figured what the heck, why not? I left out one more time, letting my company know this would be my last trip. The days were going slow and I couldn't wait to get home. I was definitely nervous to leave my job and start something new as well as be around a woman the entire time and only one woman, which would all be firsts but I thought I loved her and I would try to do what I could to make it right. A few days before I was to come home, I received a phone call from Latisha's sister to come home that there was an accident and Latisha was hit by a drunk driver. I continued to ask questions and found out he ran a red light and T-boned her. My heart immediately sank when I thought of the idea that she was or would die. I began to ask her if she was ok. She just told me she was at the hospital and that I needed to return home right away. I called my project manager and was on the road to the airport to go home.

CHAPTER 7

Over the next few days, I had to continue to ice my hand because of my fight on Monday. It continued to throb and by Friday it was feeling much better. Even though my hand was feeling better, the only thing that truly made me feel good I wouldn't see until Monday, which was Sheila. Also since it was Friday my father would be home, which meant that I would have to deal with him that night. This was one thing I was not looking forward to. It was the middle of the night when suddenly I was yanked from bed by arm and dragged out into the kitchen. He finally let me go in the middle of the floor where I landed with a thud. I could smell whiskey on his breath and I could see anger in his eyes. "You like to embarrass me boy, well now you will pay for it." He grabbed the chair and pulled it to him and then grabbed me, taking his belt off with his other hand. He then bent me over the chair and began hitting me with the belt. He just continued to hit me, cursing and with the sense there was no end in sight. The first hit shocked me and made me want to cry but at that point something came over me and even though I grimaced in pain, I never let out a cry. I had just held everything in and didn't say a word, which made me proud and motivated me to continue to stay quiet. He was getting madder and madder, and the belt was hitting me in the thighs, butt and my back. Before I knew I was lying on the floor and it was morning. I most have passed out from the pain at some point when I was getting beat. I went to get up and pain began shooting through my body. I looked up and my mom was coming out of the bedroom and looked at me in shock and began to tear up. She finally reached me and helped me to my feet. She then proceeded to help me to the bathroom where I began to take off my shirt. I flinched because of the pain. My shirt was sticking to my back because of the cuts and blood. I had to stop removing my shirt several times due to the increased pain from the shirt pulling on my wounds. My mom took over, taking the shirt off and taking her time. Once it was off, she threw it on the floor. I looked at it and it was covered in blood. She took off my pants and underwear, which also caused pain coming off but not nearly as bad as the shirt. My mom began cleaning me up with a wet rag, just dabbing it on my back trying not to cause too much pain, every couple of minutes rinsing the rag and ringing out the blood into the sink. Once she got me all cleaned up, she headed to the bedroom to get me some clothes. When she left, I turned and looked at my back in the mirror. My back was all red with cuts and swollen all over. My butt and thighs were also red and swollen but there weren't any cuts, which I figure was because of my jeans. As Mom was about to go the bathroom I heard another door shut. It could have been my brother but he usually sleeps in so it must have been my father. Then suddenly I saw him and hatred was the only thing I felt. My mom turned toward him and told him to get out and never come back. He looked at her like she was crazy.

"You're kicking me out because of this piece of shit? Where would you get any money to take care of things or to buy your drugs?"

"I don't know but get out or I'll call the police!"

"You will be crawling back to me within a month."

"Don't bet on it. Get out!"

He looked at her with a smile and turned away to grab a beer and continued back to the bedroom. He grabbed his clothes and a few items and left. This would mean no money coming in and my brother and I would be responsible for all the chores. Luckily we had enough wood for at least the winter coming since we had been cutting, splitting and stacking wood all summer long. I was hoping that I would never see him again but I knew that I would. The rest of the weekend I lay around resting and trying to heal. It felt good not to have to work all weekend. My brother and sister didn't quite understand what was going on and I didn't tell them what happened. I just told that that Father was going to be gone awhile at work. They waited on me all weekend since my mom told them I was sick and needed some rest. It made me feel good that they cared about me and were taking care of me. The next week went by very slow. We saw Mom more than usual due to the fact she had no drugs but she was also acting strange and yelling a lot more. Sheila would have some drugs such as marijuana and pills but that would only calm her for a while. I was also very sore and healing very slowly from my beating. By the end of the week, most of the pain was gone and everything except a few cuts on my back were healed. I was happy that my father wouldn't be home that weekend and things were a lot better overall around the house. Even though Mom was more intense, she was still around and there was less fighting and screaming. The weekend and the following week was the same until Friday night. I woke up to Mom talking and crying. I walked into the kitchen and saw my father standing in the living room. I was hoping I was having a nightmare and would wake up soon, but I didn't. I continued living the nightmare. I went back to my bedroom and tried to listen.

"Kelly, the only reason you want me back is for the money so you can get food and drugs, which I don't care about but you will continue to stay out of my business and how I raise the kids. Do you hear me?"

"Yes, Sam. I agree. I am sorry."

"Kelly, you are so despicable but I love you."

Then I heard a door shut and I fell back to sleep. When I got up the next morning, my father and mom were sitting at the table. As soon as they saw me, Mom got up and started cooking breakfast. Then Father called me over to the table.

"How are you feeling, Sammy?"

"I am good, Father."

"I didn't mean to punish you so bad but I was drunk and got carried away. Do you understand?"

"Yes, Father. I will try and be better."

"I hope so because if you don't you will get the belt again."

"Ok, Father."

I knew deep down he didn't really care. He was trying to save his butt so that I wouldn't tell anyone about the incident. Life at home continued as normal after that. The rest of my sixth-grade year went pretty good with no major problems. I got in a little trouble from time to time but nothing my father would find out about. During the sixth grade was the first time I smoked a cigarette, kissed a girl my own age and smoked my first joint. At home I would still receive a backhand or a kick to the gut from time to time to keep me in check when I would mess up or talk back, but none of them ever reached the level of the last. Then junior high came and the trouble, girls, drugs and fighting really began. I tried out for the football team and started lifting weights after school. I figured by playing football I could impress my father and some girls. But after a few weeks I got mad and threw my helmet at my coach and it hit him in the nose, busting it and causing blood to go everywhere. So I was kicked off the team. I kept lifting weights figuring that it would help me in the long run and help me defend myself against my father or anyone else. I started hanging out with a different group of kids that were known to be troublemakers but they were just like me and we got along great. Over the next year, I would try all kinds of things. I started drinking alcohol and smoking more weed. It made me feel so good and made me forget all my problems at least for a bit. My buddy's parents smoked marijuana so he would steal some as much as he could. We would also pool our money to buy a bag from time to time. Most of the kids in my neighborhood were around the same age and we would get together where there was any spare time. One night we were all hanging out at James's house, which was about two miles away. I had ridden my bike over there. We had been playing some football when James's brother got home. He was a couple of years older than us but we all hung out together. Once he made it over to us he showed us a bag of weed he just got. We all decided to go next door to another friend's house. Her name was Tiffany. We were pretty good friends and would hang out a lot at school and anytime possible. We all got to her place where she met us outside by her pond, which was down beyond the hill in the backyard. Joey, James's brother, pulled out the bag of weed and some Zig Zags and began to roll a couple of joints. We passed around the joints and as usual I coughed several times on my first hit. Joey and thee guys started laughing as Joey slapped me on the back. We were all feeling pretty good by the time we smoked them both. Tiffany and I were sitting there talking when she leaned over and whispered in my ear.

"Let's go have sex."

I was very surprised but very excited. I had a crush on Tiffany for a while and we had been friends for a long time. I slapped Joey on the shoulder and told him we would be back in a bit. We snuck off behind some trees where we had sex. She wasn't a virgin and neither was I since I had been with Sheila. I was a lot more experienced than she was and you could tell. It wasn't like being with Sheila but it was still a lot of fun. Afterward, we returned to the other guys where they had another joint rolled and ready. The rest of the night Tiffany and I were attached and I thought this meant we were a couple but I was wrong. A few days later she was all over Joey and they were officially seeing each other. I was pissed off at them both for a while but I got over it as soon as he pulled out a huge bag of weed. We continued to be good friends and hung out from time to time but slowly grew distant. Tiffany began to have a lot of problems that we could not help her with. I was always trying to find the next high or buzz. It was a way to release my feelings, just like fighting did but in a different way. Another night I was staying at my buddy's house and trying to figure out how we could get some alcohol. Then he remembered that one of his neighbors had four or five bottles of whiskey in his garage. He would go over there with his father to talk and the neighbor would always pour his father and himself a drink. We got dressed in black and ran to his neighbor's house. When we got over there everything was locked up. We ran back to the house and grabbed a crowbar from the garage and headed back over. We got to the side door and Frankie jammed the crowbar in the door and began to pull and yank. After about six pulls, the door made a loud crack. It still wasn't open though and we were afraid we may have woke someone. Finally I pushed him out of the way and in one good kick the door slammed open. We got to the cupboard and there were several bottles. We grabbed two of them: Jose Cuervo and a bottle of Canadian Mist. Then I noticed that on the counter there was a gallon-size bag full of weed. I slapped Frankie on the shoulder and showed him the weed. I gave him a smile and I grabbed the weed then we took off. Before we made it out the door, a light turned on, we freaked out and Frankie dropped the Canadian Mist on the concrete, smashing it all over. We both took off on a run and didn't look back until we got to a ditch just down the road. That's where we hid for about a half hour, making sure no one came. Then we continued to Frankie's house. His parents were away until the morning so we had the house to ourselves. Once we got back, we put the weed in my bag since we didn't have any papers and Frankie was afraid to even have it in the house. There definitely was a lot of weed and we were going to be in a lot of trouble if we got caught by the neighbor or police. We went to the table and poured two coffee cups of tequila. I took a big drink and my chest was on fire and I thought I was going to puke but I swallowed it all and told Frankie it was his turn. He took a drink and then followed by spitting it all over the kitchen. I then decided to find something to put it in and the only thing there was in the refrigerator was milk and orange juice. We grabbed the OJ and poured it with the tequila and we thought that was the best thing ever. We sat down in front of the television and started watching "South Park." After a couple of cups we were drunk and "South Park" become even funnier. We started wrestling and Frankie landed on the coffee table breaking one of the legs. We clamed down after that and started watching Showtime and a show called "Red Shoe Diaries." Frankie thought the show was the greatest show ever. He had never seen anything that showed boobs and sex. So for a while he was glued to the television. Somewhere along the way we passed out. The next thing we knew we heard someone at the door. We looked up and it was the morning and it was Frankie's parents at the door. We started fumbling and running around trying to take care of things as his parents walked in and caught us red-handed.

CHAPTER 8

As my assistant foeman was driving me to the airport, all I could think about was Latisha. Was she ok? Would I make it in time? I tried to think about something else but all I could think about was Latisha, then it was the drunk driver. *If she dies I will kill him*, I thought. We were only twenty minutes away from the airport but it felt like forever and I kept looking at the speedometer to make sure he was going at least the speed limit. Then I thought, *did I tell him everything? Will he be able to run the crew?* Well, I guess it doesn't matter at that point but he was a good guy and I didn't want to hang him out to dry. So, before we got to the airport, I went through everything again. At the end he said,

"Everything will be alright just go and take care of things and I will call you later."

"Thanks, Matt. If you need anything just give me a call, alright?"

"Don't worry about anything, that is why we have the office."

I felt relieved some and confident he would be alright. We finally got to the airport and parked in the short-term parking and Matt came in with me to help with my luggage. My stomach was turning. I couldn't even think once I got up to the counter and Matt had to do most of the talking for me. I kept drifting off and didn't know what was being asked so Matt would answer. I was able to get an emergency flight and would be home within four hours. As soon as I got to the terminal, they were making the last call for the flight so I had to hurry I just made it in time and hopped on the plane to find my seat. As soon as we were in the air and the flight attendant came by, I bought a shot and closed my eyes. It took me a few minutes to fall asleep because I couldn't get Latisha out of my mind. Once I fell asleep, the next thing I heard was the pilot announcing we were about to land and buckle up. We landed and I was filled with a lot of emotions and couldn't get off the plane fast enough. Finally, I was off the plane and hustling to baggage. Once down there, I waited for my baggage and headed straight to Hertz to get a rental. As I was getting the car, I received a call from her sister checking on where I was at. I answered the phone as I was signing the papers to the rental. Her sister sounded very upset and worried where I was. I told her I was at the airport and just about to leave with a rental and should be there within the hour. I was in flint and she was in Saginaw at the Saint Mary's trauma unit. She told me to hurry that Latisha really needed me there. I knew things were really bad but kept hope that everything was alright. I made it to Interstate 75 and headed north. I looked down at my speedometer every once in a while, making sure I wasn't speeding too much. At one time I looked down I was going ninety mph. I slowed it down a bit and set the cruise. I could not get pulled over not only because of the ticket but also because of the time it would take. Once I made it to the hospital I hurried and headed toward the entrance where I saw a few of Latisha's friends. They all gave me hugs and began to cry on my shoulder. "She's been waiting to see you," they said. They escorted me upstairs and to her room. I took one look at her and I knew it wasn't good. I was filled with anger for the guy who hit her. I walked over to the edge of the bed and held her hand. I began to talk to her, letting her know I was there and that everything would be alright. There were wires running everywhere and they had a tube in her mouth and nose. Before long the doctor came in and told us what was happening and it wasn't good. He told us it was just a matter of time before she wouldn't be able to live by herself and that the injuries were beyond repair. He told us that they had done all they could. The only thing left was for us to be there and for them to try to keep her as comfortable as they could. I knelt down and kissed her forehead. I told her how I felt and for her to hold on, that there were too many people who loved her for her not to. I held onto her hand for the next couple of hours talking to her and her family. I wasn't sure at times if she could understand me but from time to time she would squeeze my hand letting me know she was listening. At about eight o'clock that night her pastor showed up. He began to talk to us all to make sure we were all doing alright. He then prayed over Latisha and asked God to do his will. At this point in my life, I wasn't sure if there was a God and if there was I thought he must hate me. Otherwise why would I have gone through so much pain? Why would I have the opportunity to love and then have it taken from me? I didn't understand and at the moment really didn't care. I was too angry to care. I figured if there was a God he must have left me long ago. I hated the thought of thinking this way and it really brought a lot of hate in my life. I just pushed the thought aside and continued to be there for Latisha and her family. We began to take shifts so that she could get her rest but also so she would not be alone. Her sister and I took the first shift. We talked a lot about Latisha and how it was growing up with her and about Latisha and me. Her parents came in next and we went to the waiting room to get some sleep. After about a half hour later, we saw nurses moving really fast toward Latisha's room and a code blue being announced over the loud speaker. Her sister and I just looked at one another and knew what just happened. We both got up and started toward the door. We could see that it was Latisha's room and her parents were outside the room crying. By the time we made it to the room, the nurses were coming back out of the room with drained faces and we knew she was gone. The main nurse came out and said that she had passed on and if there was anything she could do to let her know. She also said we could say our goodbyes before they did anything else. We all went in two at a time and said our final words. Her sister and I went in together and after a few minutes we decided we both needed a few minutes alone with her. So I stepped out first giving her a moment. When she came out I went in. I had never cried since I was a small child but at that moment I couldn't stop. I was angry with the world, God and that drunk driver that hit her. I was finally feeling something again and it was swept away from me. I gave her my promise to get the guy who hit her and gave her a final kiss on the forehead and walked out. As I walked out, her sister and mom came over and I gave them both hugs as they cried for several minutes in my arms. Her parents and sister were going to do all the planning for the funeral. I told them if they needed anything to let me know and I would take care of it. Everything went well and she looked so beautiful up there. The service was good; there were a lot of people who came to pay their respects including the family of the drunk driver. I respected the fact that they came and had no ill-will toward them. They did not do anything to deserve what they were going through either. So I did acknowledge them and told them thanks for coming. After the funeral I called my job and told them I would not be quitting. I would like to head out as soon as possible. My boss hesitated and thought I should take some time but I didn't want to be there and be reminded of her beauty, the fun we had together and our plans for our future. He finally agreed and the next day I was off to Columbus, GA. Over the next six months, I didn't go home at all, finishing one job and heading to the next. At first I would talk to Latisha's sister every once in a while. Then it became a weekly then a daily occurrence. I enjoyed talking to her and I think she enjoyed it as well.

We both needed someone to talk to. We were in the position where we needed each other even if it was only over the phone. It gave us a release and something to look forward to, which wasn't much. It just felt good to have someone who really understood what you were feeling. We would also talk about the trial, Latisha, little about our past, and our future, what we wanted to do and how everyone else seemed to be holding up. She told me that this Jim, the drunk driver, was out on bond and that he was a lawyer and an ex-cop. He had a lot of pull and looked like his sentence was going to be soft. I hated the thought and all the pent-up anger began to pour out. I told her I would be home in a couple of days and I would talk to her then. The rest of the time went by slow and I couldn't wait to get home. I wasn't sure what I was going to do but I knew for sure me and this Jim were going to have a talk. The job finally got done late Thursday afternoon so I told the guys we would be leaving out at four o'clock on Friday morning. We drove straight through and made it back at the yard just before midnight. We unloaded and took care of all the equipment and called it a night. As I was hopping into my truck I got a brief smell of Latisha's perfume. I looked around and Helen, Latisha's sister, was standing behind me. I had given her a call earlier in the evening telling her we would be home in a few hours. I wasn't sure why she was there but it felt good to see her. As I turned around she was in my arms and the only thing I could think about was Latisha. She smelled like her, looked like her in so many ways and I hadn't been with another woman since meeting Latisha. Something inside me said it was ok no matter what happened. We both needed each other emotionally and physically, even if it was only for one night.

CHAPTER 9

Frankie's mom's jaw almost hit the floor when she walked in the door.

"What the hell do you think you are doing?"

We just stood there not knowing what to say or do. I was standing there with the bottle of Jose in my hand and Frankie was trying to get rid of the cups and munchies we had out all night.

"Where did you get that from?" she said as she took the bottle out of my hand.

"I bought it off a kid at school for ten dollars."

"What is his name?"

"Kenny." The first name that came to my mind since we just got done watching "South Park."

"What was his last name?"

"I don't know."

"What came over you, Frankie? Why are you doing these things?"

"It was my idea. Frankie didn't know anything about it until you left."

"You will not ever come over again and I will make sure your parents take care of you at home as well."

As the last word left her mouth, I felt my stomach start to turn and I felt as if I was going to throw up. I started going to the bathroom when they stopped me, asking me where I was going. I just pointed to my mouth and then I puked all over Frankie's dad. He stepped back and was so mad and I could see he wanted to yell but instead he just said, "Damn it!" Then he walked away to the bathroom. Frankie's mom made us get everything all cleaned and then made us clean the rest of the house. We had to dust, vacuum, clean dishes, laundry and anything she could come up with. My stomach and head were turning the whole time. Once we got done we both had to take showers and put on clean clothes. Once we got dressed his mom asked me for my number. We didn't have a phone at the house and I didn't want my father to find out so I gave her Sheila's number. Sheila figured out what was going on right away and played along. She told her she would be right over and would take care of the problem right away. Sheila showed up about a half hour later. As she pulled in the driveway, she honked letting me know it was time to leave. She didn't want Frankie's parents to see her face so she stayed in the car and just waved to Frankie's mom when she came out of the door. I grabbed my bag, said bye to Frankie and headed out the door, also apologizing to his parents. Once in the car Sheila just smiled and asked, "What the heck were you thinking?" I began to tell her what happened then I hesitated at first but then I told her about the marijuana. She was a little shocked at first then she winked at me and gave me a smile. We went back to her place and I pulled the bag of weed from my duffle. Sheila grabbed it and looked at it with wide eyes and a smile. We then proceeded to take half of the bag and separated it into smaller bags and decided that half of the weed is what we would sell and the rest we would smoke. After sorting and separating the seeds and stems from the marijuana, Sheila looked at me and I knew what she wanted. She took me to the bedroom and we began to have sex. Over the last year and a half, our relationship had developed from touching in the beginning to the first time we had sex to having sex or foreplay on a daily basis. I was still only twelve but Sheila treated me as if I was an adult and I liked that. After an hour or so we decided I better head home since my parents were expecting me back in the morning and it was already two o'clock. When I got home nobody was there so I headed inside and changed my clothes so that I could stack and split some wood. I knew that even though they were not home, Father would still expect to see some work done. After grabbing something to eat, I went outside and began to stack wood since we had a big stack already split. I was still feeling a little ill but after awhile I must have sweated it all out of me. I began to feel pretty good and began to work at a faster pace. I worked for a couple of hours getting it all stacked and getting ready to split some when my family pulled into the driveway. They all got out of the vehicle all happy and excited. I was happy to see my sister and brother with smiles on their faces. It made me feel better about the situation and life to see them happy. My sister ran up to me and told me how they had all kinds of fun at Chucky Cheese's and that they had McDonald's for supper. I looked to see if they brought me anything but they didn't. I asked what I was going to have for supper and my father said, "Nothing. You haven't got enough work done yet." He was correct that they didn't buy or fix me anything either. My father kept his word and my stomach was aching. I went to bed without eating but I was still happy and I wasn't going to let my father ruin that. My brother and sister had fun, I didn't get in trouble about the booze and I had all kinds of weed. It couldn't get much better than that. Father was gone before I woke on Sunday morning to get an early start to the week. I was glad to see him gone. The rest of the day we just chilled and watched television. Monday morning Sheila stopped by early to drop off the bags of weed so that I could sell them before and after school. It took me a few days but by the end of the week I had sold all sixteen bags of weed with only one sign of trouble. A punk named Tyrone tried to get away without paying and giving me some trouble about it. After a brief chat with him in the bathroom, he made the right choice to pay up. I had a wad of cash to show for my troubles and plenty of weed to smoke at home. After school, Sheila and I smoked it up after our usual routine of sex. Afterward we discussed what we should do with the money and if we should try to further our business endeavors in selling more weed. We decided to take the money, throw a party and buy some more weed to continue to sell and smoke. Our business was going well and for the most part

I was staying out of trouble. I did get into a couple of fights and had a few detentions for those fights but nothing that got me in trouble at home. Even though I wasn't getting caught for my troubles at home, the tension was still building and so was my hatred for my father. My mom was getting sicker and besides her typical drugs, she was now also taking drugs that the doctors were giving her to help with pain and her illnesses. Now, even on the weekends we didn't see Mom. Sheila was the only thing really keeping us fed and in proper order. Even when Father came home on the weekends we counted on Sheila since he was too drunk to really do much of anything. Things just began to get worse it seemed. By the middle of winter, Mom never got out of bed unless to use the bathroom and at times she didn't even get up for that. There were doctors and nurses that would come in from time to time but nothing was ever told to us kids about her condition. One day I asked Sheila what was going on with her. Sheila finally told me she had cancer and eventually neither the doctors or the medicine would do anything. It was just a matter of time and that the doctors were just doing whatever they could to keep her comfortable. Things stayed like this for about a year and then one day when I got home from school there was an ambulance and police cars at my house. My mom had died and they were getting ready to leave when I got there. I was overwhelmed with emotion but all I could think about was my brother and sister. I ran inside and my brother and sister were both crying and Sheila was taking care of them and trying to answer questions for the cops. I had detention that day and so they got home before I did.

Sheila said that she had died in her sleep and that she had been in a lot of pain. Sheila agreed that she would take care of us all until everything got figured out. The police agreed and left us with Sheila until the courts and child services made a decision. My father hurried home once he got word of my mother but after the funeral, social services declared my father unfit to take care of any of us. My mom's sister Barbara said she would take us in but I did not want to go. After some time, social services agreed to let my aunt have custody of us all. I talked my aunt in letting me stay with Sheila. She agreed and I was able to stay with Sheila for as long as the courts saw fit and everyone involved agreed to the terms of the court. Aunt Barbara wasn't happy about it but understood I didn't want to leave my school, which is what I told her and not the fact that I didn't want to lose Sheila, the only one I felt that actually cared for me, or seemed to anyway. A lady from the state was there when we each got our stuff and headed to our new homes. I gave my brother and sister hugs and watched as they drove off both crying and looking back at me. It was the best thing for them both; it put them out of harm's way from father and Sheila. Even though I wanted to be with Sheila, I didn't want them to be with or around Sheila. We all promised to call all the time and we could see each other on the weekends and holidays when possible. I would watch my father's place, checking up on him trying to make sure everything was alright with him. From time to time, I would go over there and stack and split wood during the week when he wasn't around. I kind of felt sorry for him and wished things were different. Once in high school, I began to party a lot more. We would have parties at Sheila's house, smoking marijuana and drinking until we dropped. High school started off as a blur. I would see my father from time to time and it seemed he was really sick and I was told he wasn't driving a truck any longer either. A couple of years went by and I was entering the eleventh grade and a girl named Stacy moved to town to live with her stepsister Lisa. She was a year younger but in the same grade as us and was in a couple of my classes. We hit it off right off the bat and we started hanging out after school and I started taking her to parties. Sheila hated it and at times would go crazy on me but I just brushed it off. I also heard my father was dying from kidney failure. I felt sad for him but also I felt a little relief to know he would be out of this world soon. One day as I was driving by, I saw the ambulance there at his place. I decided to stop to see what was happening and they had him on a stretcher carrying him out. Once he was out I walked over to him. He looked up at me as he passed, "You are a loser, son, and always will be. You are a disgrace and I thought this about you the day you were born. You just have no guts; your Momma made you a pansy."

Then he looked away and they carted him off. I was a little taken off guard but I should have been prepared because that was the way he was. That was the last day I would see him. A couple of days later he died in the hospital. I didn't go to the funeral but I heard there were very little people there. My brother and sister went and later that day we ate supper together. They were both growing up so fast and doing well in school. Aunt Barbara was making them into great kids. They had good grades and played in several sports. I was very proud of them and I tried to tell them as often as I could.

CHAPTER 10

Helen and I had finally made it back to her place. We had drove separately to her place and the whole way there I was thinking of stopping and going somewhere else but she smelled so good and I was in need of touching a woman. I kept going back and forth with myself. I was relieved when we got to her door knowing she was going to be in my arms very soon. As soon as the door shut, she was all over me and it felt so good. She led me to the bedroom where she threw me on the bed. She began to take off her clothes in a sexy way that was too much for me to handle I had to have her now. She finally jumped on top of me and we began to kiss very heavily then she proceeded down my neck to my chest where she ripped off my button-down shirt. I began to kick off my boots as she worked her way down. She then removed my pants and I began to breathe a little harder. She moved back up to my mouth as we began to roll all over the bed just caressing one another. It was as if Latisha was there and that was all I could think about and at one time I called her Latisha. I don't know if she heard me but she didn't respond. The rest of the night lasted forever and I didn't want it to end. It felt too good to end and I hadn't felt this good in a long while. The sun was coming up as were getting ready to go to sleep. I slept a few hours and slowly crawled out of bed trying not to wake Helen. I proceeded to get dress and head out the door to my truck never waking Helen up. Once I got back to my buddy's place, I took a shower and got into some clean clothes. I decided to make some breakfast when my buddy came in with the newspaper and threw it on the table. Once breakfast was done cooking, we sat at the table discussing the night before. He was a little shocked who it was but also happy that it happened. He knew I needed someone and so did she, especially during these tough times. After breakfast, I grabbed the paper and began to read all the headlines just browsing the paper. I got to page four where the headline read hero ex-cop looking at two to four years. The rest of the article was making Jim out to be a saint and how if he went to jail it would be an injustice. At least that is how I took it. I thought, *what about Latisha?* I thought, *even two to four years is not enough.* I was angry and getting angrier by the moment. I threw down the paper and walked away. Then the phone rang and it was Helen. I answered the phone a little leery of what to say or what was going to be said.

"Good Morning, Helen."

"Where did you go this morning? Why didn't you wake me up?"

"I didn't want to bother you."

I then told her that I read the paper and that it was a bunch of crap. I told her that it predicted he would receive two to four years, if he gets that, and that it was not justice for Latisha. We talked a while then decided to meet up later for supper. I wasn't sure what Helen had in mind about us. This kind of worried me but at the same time it felt good to be around her and talk to her. We meet for supper and enjoyed the evening together. She had the next couple of days off so we headed to her place after eating. The next couple of days we spent together at her place. We discussed the trial, she cooked and we just enjoyed each other's company. It felt good but there was some unsettled business that was still not taken care of and that was Jim, this ex-cop who killed Latisha. I wanted to know his story and why he chose to drive and kill her. I wanted to see remorse if anything. After spending the last couple of nights with Helen, I figured I would stay at my buddy's house on Tuesday but first I stopped off at Tony's Bar and Grill for a burger and a couple of beers. I went straight to the corner of the bar and took a seat. I hadn't been there in a while and Sally the bartender came over right away with my beer. She knew what I liked; I had been coming there for years. We had some small talk then she took my order. At the other end of the bar was a group of guys having some shots and shooting pool. At first I had paid no attention to them. I drank a couple of beers and then my food came. As I was eating, I noticed one of the guys looked very familiar but wasn't sure from where. Then it hit me; it was Jim. I had seen his photo in the newspaper. I wanted to make sure so I ended up moving to a table close to where they were so that I might hear his name. I was just about done with my beer when I heard one of the guys say, "Jim, it's your turn, you're playing me."

"Alright you rack."

By then I knew I was looking at the man who had killed Latisha. I walked back up to the bar and ordered two shots of José Cuervo and another Bud Light. Sally brought me the shots and as soon as she sat them down I was hammering them down. Then I ordered two more. She looked at me a little weird with those eyes, knowing something was wrong. She had known me for a long time and she knew when I was upset about something. As she was getting me two more shots, I started sipping on my beer and just started staring at Jim and the group of guys surrounding him. Jim seemed to carry himself the best out of the group and probably was a halfway decent fighter, but the one he was playing seemed to be the biggest threat if he was to jump in or if I thought he would be the first to fall hopefully. I sat there analyzing the situation and getting more upset as the minutes passed by. I was finished with my beer and had two shots in front of me. I slammed both shots and ordered another round. Sally gave me what I wanted. She looked at me with concern.

"You know who that is at the end of the counter, don't you?"

"Yes I do, Sally."

"Be careful and I understand but remember it won't bring back Latisha."

"I know Sally, I know."

"Just be careful. There's a lot of people who love and care for you including me."

I grabbed her hand and told her everything would be fine and not to worry. She gave me a smile and walked away. I continued to sit there and watched them have a good time. Then I heard two of them say they were leaving, leaving three of them left. I heard them wish Jim good luck and his response just made my blood boil even more. He just responded, "I have everything in the bag. If I get any time it will be in a protected paradise." I watched as the two guys left and then I finished my shots. I grabbed my beer and headed toward Jim. Once at the table, I asked if I could join the game. "Sure, why not," said Jim. I threw my quarters on the table for the next game and just started watching. I saw Sally watching from the corner of my eye. I then decided to buy a round for us all. As I was watching closer, the big guy I knew would be a problem had a few drinks and was well on his way. I noticed he was drinking whiskey and I kept two in front of him at all times. It was all business and I was going to make Jim pray for mercy before I was done. I continued buying rounds but lying off a few myself so that I would not lose my edge. After a few hours, I began to make conversation about the accident and the trail. Every once in a while, throwing in a comment that would make them get a little uneasy. Every once in a while, the big guy, who's name was Andy, looked angry and ready to fight by now. I would just play it off and continue shooting. Finally he had enough and got into my face. I acted as if I wasn't looking for a fight and apologized. I tried to get them stupid so that I could have more of the upper hand and with three guys that is a hard thing to do. He settled down a bit and walked away. I could see it in his eyes though he was ready. We played one more game and had a couple more shots before I told Jim how much I hated people like him. A couple minutes later, I saw Jim give a nod to the other guys. Out of the corner of my eye I saw Andy coming. As he got into reach, I swung my pool stick and hit him across the head, slicing open his ear. He stumbled a bit but then continued toward me. I couldn't see Jim or Mark, the third guy, and then suddenly I was hit in the lower back that brought me to my knees. I quickly recovered, realizing if I didn't I would be in a lot of trouble. I grabbed one of the pool balls and smashed it against the head of Mark. I saw his eyes roll into his head and drop and not get up again. I turned back to Andy as he grabbed me and threw me across the room and into the jukebox. I caught my breath a second then I got up ready but more cautious than before. He was moving slow from the alcohol but he was as strong as an ox. I still had the pool ball in my hand and as he came toward me I hit him between the legs, bending him over at the waist and grabbing him, then I gave him an upper cut with everything I had. He went flying backward along with several teeth. He just lay there as blood began to flow from his nose and mouth. I turned to see where Jim was and he was coming out of the bathroom. He was in shock when he saw me still standing probably assuming that I was taken care of already. I looked over at Sally and she had that worried look on her face and walked to the back out of sight. As I got closer to Jim, he pulled a knife on me and began to swing it. He got me on the third try across my stomach. I then went at him grabbing his arm and wrestling to the floor. I then began to slam his arm against the floor until he dropped the knife. The knife went sliding across the floor and I pinned Jim's arms down with my knees and began to hit him with everything I had. I can't remember how long I was hitting him because I blacked out somewhere while hitting him. The next thing I remember was hearing Sally's voice telling me to stop. I stopped looked up at Sally then down at Jim. There was blood everywhere. It was all over the floor, my hands, my shirt and even my face was covered in blood and Jim was no longer breathing. I had killed him.

CHAPTER 11

Now with my father gone there was no one to keep the house up and I did not want to either. So I talked to Aunt Barbara about selling the house since my mom had made her the keeper of the will and Father had not changed it either because he didn't care or was too lazy to do so. She agreed to sell the house and separate the profits three ways for each of us. It didn't take long and the house was sold. She took the money for my brother and sister and put them in accounts for college. I took my money and put most of it in an account for later use and used some to have a huge party at Sheila's. There must have been one hundred and fifty people there. We had all kings of alcohol, weed and drugs you could think of. I invited Stacy to the house too. It was the first time Sheila and Stacy would be in the same room let alone face to face. I introduced them both and walked away. I later came back and they were still talking and laughing. As much as Sheila was jealous, I was surprised but happy at what I saw. I never did tell Stacy the truth about mine and Sheila's relationship and I don't think it really mattered much. Sheila knew that I was starting to have feelings for Stacy and after that night she seemed to be alright with it. The next two years were a blur. Stacy and I started spending more and more time together even though her parents hated me and didn't want Stacey to see me. She would tell them she was going to a girlfriend's house to study or whatever she could to get out of the house. I was able to stay out of trouble for the most part. I did receive a speeding ticket and a MIP but I didn't get into any major trouble with the law. By the time our senior year hit, Stacy was talking about marriage, kids and the whole family idea. I couldn't really see myself only being with one woman the rest of my life. I did care for Stacy though but even now when tempted at parties and when she's not around I fall for it every time. I always end up having sex with another woman at the party. The other thing that bothered me was having kids. I didn't want any kids and I told Stacy that and she understood and told me she wasn't able to have kids naturally anyway. She also told me I would have to get her parents blessings and I knew that would never happen. I started thinking about things and one day I decided to go over to her place and talk to her dad. As I pulled into the driveway, my stomach was in knots. The knots weren't there because of her parents but because I was of the idea that I was about to propose. I was actually asking her parents to marry their daughter. I hopped out of my truck and headed for the house when her dad stepped out onto the porch before I could even make it to the steps. My truck is a little loud so he probably heard me coming in.

"Stacy is not here, Sam."

"I'm actually her to talk to you, sir." He looked at me a little puzzled.

"Why are you here to see me, Sam? What, do you need money for drugs or are you in some kind of trouble with the law?"

"It's nothing like that, sir."

"How much will it cost me to get you out of Stacy's life?"

"I don't know, sir. How much are you willing to pay?"

"What will it take, Sam?"

"Well, sir, how about fifty thousand dollars?"

"That's a lot of money, Sam, but if that's what it takes my daughter is worth it. If that is all it takes to get rid of a worthless punk like you, then so be it.

They had a lot of money and he thought he could buy anything, but he wasn't going to buy me. He wrote me a check for fifty thousand dollars. As he handed it to me he told me to stay away. I looked at the check then at him. Then I ripped it up in several pieces and gave it back to him.

"I am not for sale, sir. I came here to have you bless our marriage but I see this won't happen. I'll let Stacy know how you feel."

As I said this, Stacy came from around the corner.

"You don't have to explain I heard everything. I will be marrying Sam and I will be moving out as soon as possible."

"You can't do that, young lady."

I am eighteen now I can do as I please and you can't stop me."

About a month later, I pulled out some cash from the house sale and bought Stacy a ring. Then at Christmas I proposed to Stacy at Sheila's house. Sheila was very excited for us and wanted to help plan the entire thing. After Christmas, Stacy packed all her stuff where her parents were gone and moved in with me and Sheila. When her parents went home they were furious and threatened to call the cops. I'm not sure on what charges but either way they never did anyway. We both graduated, her with honors and me barely getting by not because of my smarts but because I chose to be other places instead of school most of the time. Shortly after, we graduated we got married. Sheila helped plan the entire thing and luckily she did otherwise it probably would not have been so big. Stacy looked beautiful in her dress and both my brother and sister were in the wedding. Afterward we had a huge party out to Sheila's where we had a pig roast, bonfire, horseshoes, volleyball and a DJ. There was also all kinds of alcohol to go around. It was a great time and everyone seemed to be happy, although Stacy was a little sad because her parents, especially her father, did not show up. She was hoping they would see her on the wedding day. I had used the rest of the money in the bank for a down payment on a three-bedroom ranch house with a garage and a pole barn setting on ten acres. We were going to move in there right after our honeymoon. We took the money from the weeding and headed to Niagara Falls for a three-day weekend.

When we arrived back I took Stacy to our new house and I headed to Sheila's to get all of our stuff loaded. Once I got there, Sheila had all our stuff already packed for us. It took awhile and some manueving but I got everything loaded on the truck. I headed inside where Sheila was sitting at the table and in tears. I wasn't sure what was going on so I sat down beside her and waited a bit to say anything. Then she told me she was leaving and that she can't stay around there anymore. She told me how happy she was for me and that she knew this day would come. She said she was going back to Detroit and selling the house from there and that she would be gone by next weekend. I had mixed feelings about it all. This was the woman that had basically raised me since I was five but also the same woman I had also had sexual relations with since I was five. A relief was lifted off me to know she would be leaving but also a sense of security was gone. I didn't say much about this to Stacy until a few days later so that she wouldn't call Sheila while she was upset. We both went over the next weekend and helped her pack and load her stuff. We all said our goodbyes and Sheila was out of my life forever. I wasn't sure how to think or feel but I just kept it to myself and moved on. Stacy decided to go to college and become a nurse at the local college. I was still working for an auto parts store and times were getting tough. We were living pay check to pay check and I hated that. I started to search for a better-paying job. This would also allow Stacy to concentrate on college and less on work and bills. I finally received a phone call from a pipeline engineering company. I got the job and began working right away but this job also meant travel and time away from Stacy. She was alright with it especially once I got my first couple of paychecks.

CHAPTER 12

"I called Helen; she is waiting for you outside," Sally said. I was still a little stunned and slow to react. Finally it dawned on me and headed for the door. "Once you are gone a few minutes I will call the cops and good luck," Sally said. As I walked outside, I noticed the headlights of Helen's car. It was pouring outside and as I ran to the car I could see the blood washing off my hands and the rest of my body. As I got to the car I could see Helen's eyes and she had been crying. I got into the car and she gave me a huge kiss. After a few minutes of holding me and squeezing me like she would never see me again, she finally let go. She put the car in reverse and backed out of the parking spot. Before we could make it out of the parking lot, she was trying to scheme up a plan. She wanted to know what happened and how it all happened. While I was telling her she noticed I was bleeding a bit from my stomach and was concerned right away. I told her what happened and her face showed concern and that she was afraid. I ensured her everything was going to be alright. I told her everything from buying the shots to Sally waking me from my blackout. I told her I would not run that I would deal with the consequences of my actions. In the back of my mind I was hoping for a self-defense plea but knew it would be tough considering the evidence. I told Helen everything would be alright and continued to try to reassure her of that. My hand was beginning to throb and I knew it was probably broken. I asked Helen if she had anything for pain in the car. She told me there was Tylenol in the glove compartment. I took four Tylenol and tried to close my eyes and forget the pain but that wasn't going to happen. As we pulled into Helen's driveway, I could see she wanted to say something so I waited for her to speak.

"I want you to know how much I care for you and how I want everything to be alright. I am also having mixed feelings because of the fact you were with my sister. I also understand why my sister was in love with you because I am starting to feel the same way."

I wasn't sure what to say other than reassure her again that everything would be alright. We finally made it inside and I had to take a shower and get into some clean clothes. Helen had some clothes left over from her old boyfriend that she brought to me while I was in the shower. The pain in my hand was going away for now but while in the shower I realized I was cut pretty good across my stomach. It really wasn't too deep but the running water made the pain a little worse. After the shower, I looked through the cupboards and drawers to find a bandage. Once I found one I put it on because I didn't think the cut was that bad to where I needed stitches. After getting all bandaged up, I got dressed and headed to the kitchen where Helen was. She was cooking some breakfast for the two of us. I sat down as she made our plates. We sat there looking out into space not saying a word. As soon as we finished, Helen broke down into tears.

"I can't believe this is all happening but at the same time I expected something would happen."

"Everything will be ok," I kept telling her. "Let's just enjoy the next few hours and deal with it in the morning."

As we were leaving the kitchen, she looked up at me with those seductive eyes and led me to the bedroom. Over the next hour, we enjoyed each other's bodies. The cut on my stomach was definitely hurting but I wasn't going to let that stop me from enjoying every pleasure Helen had to offer. Afterward, as we lay in bed in each other's arms, I felt a sense of relief. I knew that in the morning things would get a little crazy but I was savoring the moment. Morning came and we slowly rolled out of bed. I was very sore from my head to my feet. I went to the bathroom to check on my cut. I knew it had been bleeding but I wasn't sure how much. As I took off my shirt, the bandage tore off with my shirt. The blood had gone through my bandage and was sticking to my shirt. I cleaned my cut and put on a new bandage. Helen got me another shirt to put on and I went to my cell phone to see if anyone had called. I had fifteen messages from everyone including Tommy, Rebecca, Sally and Bob, my buddy. Bob left a message saying that the cops stopped by looking for me and asking questions where I was and when I would be home. Tommy and Rebecca were both worried saying that I was a fugitive on the run. That is what they had on the television that morning. They also said that they wanted me to turn myself in as soon as possible. I deleted all my messages and went to find Helen. When I got to Helen she was watching the news and they were talking about the incident and saying that I brutally killed Jim based on revenge and that I was considered dangerous. I looked at Helen and told her that I would need her to drop me off at the police station so that I could turn myself in. I also signed over my truck to her so that it wouldn't be taken for fees or whatever the courts might come up with. She gathered up her things and we headed out the door. We didn't say anything on the way there. I just continued looking out the window thinking about what was ahead of me. As we pulled up near the police station, I looked at Helen and she looked very stressed.

"I am sorry for everything just stay strong. I promise everything will be alright."

I could see tears beginning to form again in her eyes as see leaned toward me and wrapped her arms around me. We stayed that way a few moments Then I pulled away and gave her a kiss.

"I will see you soon," I told her, "just let everyone know that I am alright."

I stepped out of the car and instantly a knot formed in my stomach. I hesitated a moment then kept going straight into the police station. I walked up to the counter and announced who I was and that I was there to turn myself in. Two officers immediately came out the door and put me into handcuffs. They read me my rights as they were taking me to the back to be processed. The one officer kept giving me the eye and I knew he would like to rough me up some but the other officer was luckily there to keep the peace for now. They proceeded to fingerprint me and take my picture before throwing me into a cell. After they put me into the cell, the officer who surely hated me looked at me with hate in his eyes.

"Jim was a good friend of mine and you will pay for his death."

I had requested a court-appointed attorney since I couldn't afford anything else and didn't want to ask for anyone's help. He arrived a couple hours later. He was very young and must have been straight out of college. I didn't mind though all attorneys need to start somewhere and maybe he will be a great one. I kept my faith that everything would be alright. We talked a while and I told him my story of what happened, leaving out Helen and the fact that Sally called her. I didn't want either one dragged into the situation any more than they had to. Just as we were finishing up, two officers came and said I was to be questioned now by the detectives on the case. They put me in handcuffs and shackles and took me to the interrogation room. My attorney told me to say nothing, that he would handle everything and for me to just relax. As we got into the room, the officers began to question me about the situation and what happened that night. My attorney took control and said I would give a written statement of what happened that night but that it was self-defense and not murder like they were claiming. The officers agreed that I could write a statement but was not pleased that they could not have their way with me. After a couple of hours, I was returned back to my cell. At around three o'clock they brought me some food that I wouldn't feed my dogs. I didn't touch a thing on the plate and slid it back out of my cell back into the walkway. A few minutes later, two officers came to the cell.

"So you don't want to eat. We try to be nice and you treat us like this. Maybe we need to teach you a little respect."

They unlocked the cell and came on in, shutting the door behind them. I was still in shackles but didn't have any handcuffs on. The first officer was the same one who earlier I could see wanted to put a hurting on me. He grabbed his bayonet and swung it, hitting me across my arm then he jabbed me in the guts, bringing me to my knees. The other officer put handcuffs on me. I tried to struggle but I got hit again across my back. They finally got the cuffs on me and they made sure they were as tight as possible. They began to take turns hitting me everywhere besides my face. At one point I felt one of my ribs break. After a while the pain became a burning sensation then I was numb to the pain. After several minutes of taking the blows, the officers were getting angrier and hitting me harder. They wanted me to scream out but I wouldn't make a sound. I finally collapsed to the floor. After a couple of kicks to the side, they removed my handcuffs and left me lying on the floor. I wasn't able to move and after a while I stopped trying. I started thinking about my life and all that had happened and all the things I had done wrong. The next thing I knew I was being tapped to wake up. It was my lawyer. He gave me his hand as I struggled to get up. He led me to the bed where I sat there a moment to catch my breath. I was having a hard time breathing and was in a lot of pain. I told my lawyer what had happened. He left the cell and returned with the officer on duty. They began to look me over and then called for an ambulance. At the hospital they said I had a collapsed lung and several broken ribs. I also had a broken left arm. I would stay in the hospital for the following week with an armed guard outside my door. The police were claiming that my allegations were false and that my injuries came from the brawl. At that point I knew what I was up against and couldn't count on anyone. I was on my own and I was fighting an uphill battle. The police wouldn't allow any visitors in my room, only ones in or out were doctors and nurses. After returning to my jail cell, I passed the officers who had given me that beating. They just gave me a smile as I was being escorted back to the holding area. I was there only a few minutes when my lawyer showed up. He explained to me since you were not examined by a medical provider that these injuries are being claimed to be from your fight and that I had no leg to stand on to claim otherwise. He kept saying how he believed me but there was nothing that could be done at that point. He also told me my arraignment date was set where I would enter my plea against my changes. He then proceeded to tell me what exactly they were charging me with. The list was quite long. They were trying to get me for everything they could; the list included second-degree murder, assault and battery, fleeing and multiple smaller crimes such as public intoxication, public disorderly and eight charges in all. I would go before the judge in a week.

"How would you like to plea?" Frank asked.

"I will plead not guilty, Frank."

"That is what I figured and would suggest but we also cannot allow this to go to trial because you will lose so we must begin to think about a plea bargain. You need to start preparing mentally that you are going to go to prison for some time."

"I am prepared for what happens and I am ready for whatever might happen."

I already figured this and I knew he was just trying to tell me everything and he seemed to want to do his best even with little experience, and I appreciated that. We shook hands and he left saying he was going to try to find a way to get me a minimum and lower sentence. I didn't see him again until our first court date. As I was escorted down the hall to the courtroom with shackles and handcuffs on, he was waiting for me at the door of the courtroom. As I got to him, he asked me how I was holding up and that he would brief me once we got inside. As I was getting ready to sit down, I saw Helen come into the room. I told Frank she was there and he went and greeted her and escorted her to the row behind me. There was already a group of people on the other side and several of them crying. I hated seeing them cry but I had no regrets about what happened that night. Certainly, I wished things were different and that I wouldn't have killed him but it was what it was. Frank looked at me and told me what would happen and how to respond. He said this would be really quick and another date would be set to hear the evidence. The judge entered the room and the bailiff told us to rise then we were all told to sit as the judge sat. The judge went over the paperwork then began to speak of the case.

"Mr. Jones, please stand for the court. Do you understand the charges and how do you plea?"

"Sir, I understand the charges and I plea not guilty to all charges."

"Ok, Mr. Jones. Take your seat."

The courtroom began to get loud and a lot of the people behind the prosecutor were calling me a murderer. How could I plea not guilty? The judge slammed his gauntlet and the court went quiet again. I sat down and began to think about what my father had said. That I was nothing and always will be nothing. *Maybe he was right*, I thought. As I sat there in my own little world, I heard all rise. I stood up and the judge left the courtroom. I looked at Frank and asked what he said as I was not there for a moment. He summarized what was said and that he would get back to me when a date would be set. As we got up the officers came over to take me back to my cell. I looked at the crowd of people behind the prosecutor and received several looks that would kill me if looks could kill. I knew they were hurting but so were we and I felt for them but not Jim at all. I was glad he was dead. I was still filled with hate for that man and what he had done to Latisha and had taken from me. I then looked at Helen as she had tears rolling down her face. I reached out to her and felt her hand against mine when one of the officers knocked my hand away. I looked back to her as I was leaving and she broke down and started crying even more. I hated seeing

Helen cry for me. She had already been through so much I didn't want to hurt her anymore.

CHAPTER 13

Helen was able to come see me every Sunday for an hour. She was always there and it was something I looked forward to and got me through each week. I had got my next court date so now it was just a waiting game. I had about another month until my next court date and we were hoping that shortly after that we would hear a plea bargain that was worthy enough to accept. Frank had already been talking to the prosecutor but at this point they were unwilling to cooperate. As we got closer to the court date, Frank began briefing me on what I was going to say and what I was not going to say. He also had written statements from Sally, Helen and statements from character witnesses such as Bob and Matt. Finally, the court date was upon us and I was as ready as I could be. No one was allowed into the courtroom except the lawyers, judges and me. No outside interruptions would be allowed. When I got to the courtroom, I thought Helen was waiting for me with Frank. The officers escorted me to a room along with Frank and Helen to discuss how things would go and to walk me through everything one more time. Helen sat right next to me the whole time, hanging onto my head and reassuring me instead of me reassuring her that everything would be alright. Frank turned away and gave me and Helen a few minutes. We embraced one another and it felt so good to have her close to me. I wished that moment wouldn't go away but we had to get into the court we gave each other a kiss and she grabbed my hand as I stood up. I looked down at her and for the first time ever I told a woman that I loved her. I felt what I thought was love with Stacy and Latisha but never told them and I wasn't going to make the same mistake again. Helen kind of looked at me and told me she loved me too and that she loved hearing me say that. As I walked away, her hands slowly slid out of mine and then me and Frank walked out the door. There were a lot of different angles going on with this case because of all the different circumstances. There was Latisha, the fact that Jim was an ex-cop and stories not matching up. Also the fact that Michigan had no death penalty laws and the fact that corruption was hovering over the police department that was looking over my case. As I walked into the courtroom, my hands began to sweat a bit and I started to get really nervous. I looked at Frank and he must have felt the same way because he was sweating bullets. We made it to the front to our seats and sat down. We looked at one another, taking deep breaths.

"Are you ready, Sam?"

"I can't get anymore ready, Frank."

Then suddenly the judge came out.

"All rise," the bailiff announced.

"Everyone take your seats. Does either party have any concerns or questions that need to be addressed before we get started?"

"No," Frank said.

"No," the prosecutor responded.

"If no one has any problems then is all evidence and statements turned in?"

"Yes," both parties responded.

"Alright then let's get this process started."

Over the next couple of hours, I was harassed about my story and I stuck to what I said while the prosecutor tried to trick me from time to time. Officers were sworn in to tell what they saw at the crime scene. The other two guys there that night also testified as to what happened. Then Sally and Helen were called in to testify as well. As each party was called in, they were sworn in. They were all approached by both Frank and the prosecutor and then told to take a seat and be ready if there were any more questions for them. Each person was brought into the court individually so that the story of each told was not influenced by what they heard. After all the evidence was heard, the judge called for a recess for two hours to go over the statements and evidence again. During the recess the prosecutor and Frank discussed the case and options for about a half hour but not coming to an understanding. Frank was trying to get me the best deal possible and believed the prosecutor would be happy with a much lesser plea if it presented itself. We all returned to the courtroom where the judge made his decision. He told the court that there was enough evidence to go to trial. He said most of the evidence is clear and concessive but that most of it was circumstance and that a jury could go either way. He dismissed the court saying he would set a date for trial but that he wanted to see both parties in his office. Frank said that the judge thought it was best for both sides and the county if this didn't become a circus and was settled before trial. Frank told them we would plea guilty if the charges were lessened but that the prosecutor was unwilling to budge. He said that the prosecutor left saying he needed a couple of days and he would get a hold of Frank. This made me feel a lot more confident about my chances. It certainly wasn't what I wanted but it would be better than second-degree murder. After about a week, Frank came to me and said the prosecutor would agree to a manslaughter charge and everything else would be dropped. Frank said I was looking at about ten years depending on the judge's decision. I hated the fact that I could be looking at this many years but the alternative could be worse. So I agreed that I would plead guilty to manslaughter. I also knew that Frank had never taken a case to trial and that my chances would decrease if we took the chance. The processes took place and after a short while I was in the courtroom again with Helen sitting behind me, but this time I would be pleading guilty to manslaughter and hauled away to prison. I took a quick glance at Helen and then back to the judge as he told me to rise.

"I see that we have agreed to a plea of manslaughter. Do you understand these charges?"

"Yes, sir."

"How do you plea, Mr. Jones?"

"I plead guilty, sir."

"You are of your own free will and understand what this means?" the judge asked.

"Yes I do, sir."

"A plea of guilty has been entered for manslaughter for the case of Sam Jones vs. the state of Michigan in the death of Jim Burns on the night in question. Therefore, Mr. Jones will serve a term of no more than ten years and no less than two years in a maximum security prison. This case is adjourned."

He slammed down the gauntlet and got up. "All rise." We rose and as the judge walked out I turned to Helen and we put our arms around one another and I gave her a kiss.

"Just stay strong. I will see you soon," I told her.

I turned to Frank, shook his hand and told him thanks. By then the officers were in front of me with the handcuffs to take me away. The two officers began to handcuff me and put my shackles on when a woman came over. I think it was his sister or some other close relative and slapped me across my face.

"You'll go to hell for this," she said.

The one officer grabbed her and told her to go and that any more incidents she would also go to jail for contempt of court. The next morning I was awakened by a baton being run down my cell.

"Here's your last breakfast from here. You leave for Ionia's maximum facility prison in two hours."

I grabbed the tray and began to eat my soggy eggs,

burnt toast and bacon. As I sat there eating, I looked up and saw Helen. Boy was I happy to see her. I told her were I was headed and she already knew. Frank had called her and let her know earlier that morning. The officer allowed us some free time together as he walked away a bit. It was nice to just talk to Helen alone without everyone around. After a while the officer came back and opened the cell and allowed Helen and me to have one last kiss before she had to leave. The officer told Helen it was time and I gave her one last I love you and she walked out. I thanked the officer since he didn't have to let Helen and me have out time. He just responded with, "Don't worry about it; I know what they did to you and I don't agree. I just can tell you to keep your faith. If you have any, if not find it."

"Thanks."

Then the officer walked away. As I was escorted to the care, I looked to the heavens and asked God for forgiveness and to watch over Helen and give her strength to deal with the situation. Also to give me the guidance I needed to get through my situation. I wasn't sure at the time if there was a God but if there was I wanted him on my side. I figured one day I would have the answer to this question. The next two hours I just looked out the window of the car. It felt like days instead of a couple of hours. I was then escorted by four officers to a shakedown area where I was stripped of everything and issued a new uniform and a prisoner ID number. After all the business was taken care of, I was taken to my jail cell. It was smaller than my other cell and I had to share it with another person who wasn't there at the time. I got settled in looking at some of the pictures and books that my roommate had. There was the Bible and several books dealing with the teachings of Paul, who I later found out was a prophet in the new testaments. I wasn't sure at this point if I would like my cellmate or not. I was hoping he wasn't a religious nut that would preach to me about all my wrongs, especially since we both sat in the same place. As I lay there on my bunk, a big man came to the cell. I thought maybe he was my cellmate but then he told me he was the liaison. He was to show me around the place and tell me what time chow and yard times were. As he showed me around, he told me where to stay clear of because of gangs and rival gangs that would kill you in a minute. After the tour, I was sent back to my cell to wait for chow. He also told me every night and morning there is an accountability formation. Each prisoner must stand outside his cell and be counted. If someone is not there the whole place goes on lockdown. I wasn't sure how I could adjust but I had to; there wasn't much of a choice. I was in a place where a wrong move would kill me. Every person was a threat and I couldn't trust anyone. As I lay there in my bunk, I thought how every day was a survival. I must learn the ropes but first I must find someone I could trust. Shortly after thinking this, my cellmate returned. He was a big man a little taller than me and looked like he had been in plenty of battles. He had several scars on his face and his knuckles looked like he had broken them several times. He had tattoos on the upper parts of his arms and one was on his forearm of Jesus Christ.

"So you're the fresh fish I had heard about. You're my cellmate. Just to let you know my last cellmate was killed so you might want to be careful. No, I am just kidding, he was released last week. My name is Tony. You do have to be careful though; many people do get killed here so just keep to yourself and don't look wrong at anyone in a threatening way. I will try to teach you the ropes around here and all the different gangs but the most important thing is not to make enemies but at the same time hold yourself in a way that shows you are not afraid."

"Thanks, I appreciate that. My name is Sam Jones."

This place was even more than I expected but I was up for the challenge to survive. I told myself I need to look on the positive side of everything so that I could make it out alive as well as have a good mind when I get out.

CHAPTER 14

Tony and I were getting along great and at this point I hadn't started any trouble. I had been in now for a month and Helen was going to come down and see me this Sunday. She said she had some good news and in this place good news would be great. By this time I was into a daily routine; I worked out a lot mostly in the cell doing pushups, sit-ups, pull-ups, whatever I could think of. I was also working in the laundry room, which also helped pass time. I kept to myself for the most part trying to be low key. I had started reading some of Tony's books; they were very interesting and I started asking questions about certain aspects of the Bible that Paul would talk about. Tony never pressured me but was there when I had a question. One day I asked him what had happened to him. He said he was in prison on three counts of murder. He had returned home early one day to find his wife in bed with two other guys. He killed all three and is now serving three life sentences. I couldn't imagine Tony killing anyone but he said he was a lot different now than he used to be and that in a fit of rage with no true backbone in Christ anything is possible. He had already served fifteen years and had seen many cellmates come and leave. He said that he had been in a year when his cellmate introduced him to Jesus. He said at first he thought it was hogwash but he listened and began reading the Bible and one day it all came together. He accepted Jesus as his Lord and Savior. I didn't quite understand how people like us are in a place like this could be saved or accepted to heaven. I continued to ask questions and tried to learn everything I could. Tony began to preach to me about mercy, which I didn't understand really how God could show mercy to people like me. As he continued to preach and teach me about this thought, I began to hope this was true. Could God really have mercy on me and forgive me for my sins? Tomorrow was Sunday and that meant Helen would be there. I was looking forward to her and the good news. This was the first time I had the possibility of seeing her. I didn't sleep that much that night because I was thinking about what I had read that day and I saw Tony get up as he usually did on Sunday and go and teach about Jesus. I watched as he left and I was thinking to myself I should go with him but I didn't and I stayed back. I was finally called to get up because I had a guest, which meant Helen was there. When I got to the room, Helen was seated at a bench in the corner. There were about fifteen other guys sitting around the room talking and laughing with their visitors spread across the room. I made myself to Helen and just before I got there, she stood up and wrapped her arms around me. We began talking about how each of us were doing and how we were holding up. Then she told me she had to tell me something. I was excited and concerned to find out what the good news was.

"What is it?" I said.

"I am pregnant," she said.

I didn't know what to say. I just sat there a moment. I knew what I had done when Stacy told me she was pregnant and I always wondered how everything worked out but knew the kid was better off without me. I wouldn't have the chance to hurt him as well. Many thoughts began to swirl around my head. She just looked at me waiting for a response but I didn't know what to say. I finally looked up at her and said I don't know what to say. She kind of looked upset but I didn't. I was filled with all kinds of emotions. I started to explain to her how I felt and even though she acted as if she understood, she really didn't and I could see she was upset. I didn't know what to say; I didn't want to treat Helen like I did Stacy. I knew I had made a mistake back then but couldn't correct my mistakes now, at least that was what I thought. I received good news that day but felt terrible inside and didn't know how to express my thoughts to Helen. At the end of the hour, I held onto Helen and didn't want to see her go. I wanted to tell her more but didn't know how. I knew she should know how I felt and why. I watched as she left and she said she would return during the next visitation. As I was returning to my cell, I decided to talk to Tony about my situation. I didn't know why but I began to spill my guts to Tony and he just sat there and listened. He never judged me, interrupted or thought any less of me. He gave me a good idea and that was to write down how I was feeling and why. He said maybe I should spill my guts to her like I did him. He also said that even though my father was the way he was and the things I had gone through with Mom and Sheila doesn't mean I am bad nor would do the same to my child. This was the first time he really preached to me but I understood. He told me that through Jesus Christ I could be forgiven but first also I must forgive myself and others. That living a life in shame and running from your fears was not the answer but that I must stand up and deal with every obstacle in order to take back my life from the devil. That night as I lay in bed, I began to think about what Tony said and agreed I must do something. I didn't want to get out of prison and return to the same life I once lived. I didn't want to hurt anyone anymore and I knew I had hurt a lot of people already. That Monday I began to write telling Helen everything and explaining to her how I felt and what I had done in the past. As I began to write my emotions began to flow and it was like a thousand pounds had been lifted off my shoulders, but I also had a knot in my stomach because I didn't know how Helen would react. I didn't want her to reject me or react in a way that would push another button that would case pain to me or me to cause pain to her. The following months passed and I continued to write Helen on a daily basis and she would write back. Our situation was at first a little weird but then we began to talk about things; it felt good to know she knew and continued to come back to me. Eventually she started to show and she was so beautiful. One day she came with ultrasound pictures and told me we were having a girl and for me to help think of some names. I knew immediately what her name should be.

"What about Latisha?" I said, "after her aunt?"

"I was thinking the same thing," she said.

I reinforced to her how much I loved her and that once I got out we were going to get married. She seemed very happy to hear that. Tony continued talking about the Bible, reading verses and just about everyday stuff. He began to teach me what real friendship was and what caring for someone really was. He never condemned me or questioned a thought I had. He would just listen, which I think was something I had needed for a long time. Even though I was in prison and some days it was worse than others, I had something to look forward to. One day as Tony was talking to me about the Lord, everything kind of came together and at this point I knew what Jesus had done for each of us and all the stories of the Bible since I had read it several times. I had read and listened but until that moment I didn't understand or realize what exactly it was all about. I then interrupted Tony.

"I wanted to have Jesus in my life and heart forever and I want to have salvation in Jesus."

"I am happy to you this." He looked at me with a smile.

"All you have to do is ask the Lord to forgive you and that you are truly sorry for your sins and he will enter your heart and you will live forever in the kingdom of God."

That night I prayed and asked the Lord into my heart.

It was the best feeling ever. It truly felt refreshing to know that I had a clean slate and could start over doing the things that were right rather than wrong. I knew things would still be tough and that I would have many troubles, but now I had the Lord beside me and I could talk to someone if things got too bad to handle. I'll never forget this day: it was April 2, 2005. I hadn't seen Helen in a few weeks and little Latisha was to be born any day. I couldn't wait to see her. I was actually starting to look forward to being a dad. I started thinking about the struggles Helen would have with me in here and all the responsibilities she would have to deal with. Then I started thinking of Stacy and what I had done to her and what she has and is going through raising a child by herself. One day I sat down and wrote her telling her how sorry I was and that I had no excuse good enough for leaving but I would pray she would understand. I told her how I felt and why I felt this way and prayed she would understand. It was a long shot but I also told her that I would love to see and be a part of our child's life. I told her about Helen and our baby girl. It was a detailed and long letter. I had the time to write and nowhere to go so why not get everything off my chest? I prayed every night that Helen was doing well and that God would give her the strength and courage she needed. A few more days passed and Helen and the baby were there. I was so excited to see them both. I gave them both kisses and we sat down. When I looked at them both it was unbelievable. She looked just like her Momma. Helen got her out and placed her in my arms. At first I was scared I didn't want to hurt her. It was one if not the greatest moments I had. When she left that day I knew I was a lucky man. Over the next couple of years, I continued to grow in the Lord's word and looked forward to each day even though I was in prison. That was one thing that I could relate to with Paul and that is why I think Tony could relate to him as well. We were in prison for different reasons but we were able to be reached and blessed by the Lord even in a place of prison and solitude. I was looking forward to getting out of prison and Frank was working on getting me in front of a parole board. He was now working for a firm but doing me a favor. He has been a great friend to us and hopefully it will also get me out of here. One night as I slept in bed I was awakened by several guys in my cell. Three of them had me pinned down so I couldn't move. Two other guys pulled Tony from his bunk onto the floor. They then proceeded to stab him over and over. As I laid there watching my friend die I wondered what he could have done to deserve this. I began to pray for Tony and myself. I couldn't recognize anyone but I saw a tattoo on one of the guy's forearms. It was the same tattoos that several members of a Mexican gang had on them. So I knew the group that was attacking and that was all I thought I needed. Then I heard a guard coming down the walkway and the light from his flashlight bouncing off the wall in the cell. Then the five guys took off but before they could I was able to land a punch on one of them. I knew it would leave a mark so that I could identify him later. As I got to Tony he was breathing his last breath. He was covered in blood and a puddle was forming underneath him. As I looked down at him he said, "Do not fear I am going to the Lord and I am happy. Do not allow this to affect your judgment or your relationship with the Lord. Stay strong so that you can grow and one day be with your family. Do not make the same mistakes I did and hold hatred inside me for so long. Jesus loves you."

Then he was gone. At that moment the guard made it to the cell as I held Tony in my arms. I didn't understand why something like this could happen to Tony. What did he do to deserve such a brutal death? I began to fill with hate and I was determined to fix the wrong and to take these five out of this prison the same way Tony was. What Tony had said disappeared from my mind and I was on a mission. The next day I was fired up and looking for a fight. I had been up most of the night talking to the guards and the police about what happened and what I saw. It didn't seem as if anything would be done by the police since no real evidence was present and we were criminals. They would chalk it up as another unsolved prison murder. I had forgotten what Tony had said as fast as he told me. I was not interested at the time and had my own agenda of what justice was. I began to pump myself up and make plans of how I would begin this battle. There were close to twenty of them in the yard but the only one I could make out was the one with a busted nose and a black eye. I knew he was the one I hit the night before. As I sat there filled with rage, anger and hate, I began to talk to God and asked him why this could happen. I asked him for guidance, strength and the courage I would need to continue. I wasn't mad at God but I didn't understand how everything in my life turned bad and everyone dies that I loved and for what?

Why Tony? He was a good man that loved Jesus and was dealing with his mistakes in life and only wanted to teach people about Jesus. Then I saw a guard approaching me.

"You are wanted. You have a visitor."

"Alright," I said.

I was surprised and happy. Helen said she wasn't going to make it today. She must have changed her plans. I was glad she was here; it would feel good to talk to her about Tony. She knew we were getting close and how he was teaching me. She was also excited about this just as much as I was. She had grown up in a church and had fallen away the past several years; she was looking forward to renewing her life to Christ. As I walked into the visitation room, I didn't see Helen; she wasn't at our normal table. I continued to look around then I saw her. It was Stacy. My heart was in my stomach. I was stunned to see her. As I continued to look around, there was also a little boy sitting at the table behind her. He looked just like me. I was a little scared about what was going to happen. I looked up to the heavens and asked for help to get me though this moment. As I got to the table, I could see Stacy was also nervous and worried how things would go. I sat down and told her I was glad to see her.

"Is that my son behind you?" I asked.

"Yes, that's Sam, III, I named him after you."

He looks good; you have done a great job it looks like. I am sorry for what I have done to you."

"I am here for our son and that it. He always asks about you and I always tell him you are working and maybe one day he would return." She began to cry. "Why? How could you just leave like that?"

"Did you read my letter?"

"Yes I did but we could have worked the things out."

"You're probably right, Stacy, but I was unwilling to change or to talk about my past. It has been a hard road for me and I know it hasn't been easy for you either but things are different now. I met a man in here that taught me a lot and led me to Jesus and I am trying to fix my wrongs."

She looked at me a little strange but continued listening.

"I know you don't quite understand but I have changed and even though I have changed I still have many flaws that I must continue to work on. I just want you to know how sorry I am for treating you like I did and to have a chance to show you. I want to be a part of Sam's life and actually be a dad to him. I know it will take time but when I get out I would like the opportunity to make up for my mistakes."

We continued talking and I told her about everything that had happened and about Helen and the baby. Most of it was in my letter but we talked about it some more and I showed her a picture of little Latisha. She seemed to be very happy for me. I also gave her Helen's number just in case she wanted Sam to meet Latisha. She took the number but I wasn't sure if she would actually keep it. She then called Sam over and she introduced us.

"This is Sam, Sammy."

"You have my name," he said.

"Yes I do. It's a good name, huh?"

We started talking about things he liked and what he didn't like to do. He seemed to be a very good and smart boy. Stacy has been doing a great job with him. We spent about another fifteen minutes together then the guard said it was time to go.

"It was nice to me you, Sammy, and I look forward to seeing you again. Ok."

"Ok," he said.

"Thanks, Stacy. I appreciate you coming by. I know you didn't have to do this and I know I hurt you. I wish I could take it all back but I can't, but when I get out I would love to have the chance to make it up to Sammy."

"We will see when you get out, stay strong."

They both walked away and I couldn't help but think of all the things that could have been; all the things I had missed out on. I had to change. I had to be a better father to Sammy and Latisha.

CHAPTER 15

As I was returning to my cell, I started remembering what Tony had said about the anger and hatred and I was starting to fill with both. When I got back to my cell I got on my knees and began to pray and beg the Lord for help. Tony had taught me a lot about the Bible and God's word and I remembered him speaking to me about hate and anger and how it controls our lives and kicks God to the side because we are unable to listen to the Lord beyond our anger. When I got done praying, I began to think about things; how I wanted to get out of prison and be with my family. I began to read Tony's bible and try to make sense of my situation and to try to find some guidance to get through these times. I began to read Paul's letters again to the churches. When I got to 2 Corinthians Chapter 6, I thought of Tony and the hardships we faced in prison. Paul was also enduring these same things and tells us how we must not give into those feelings of anger and hate because it separates us from God and we begin to harden our hearts. Tony would always tell me that when we begin to allow hatred to control our thoughts, we are giving into the thoughts of the devil. He used to say most of the time the other person doesn't even know or care about our feelings and our hatred only affects ourselves and begins to destroy us. I had known this feeling most of my life. I had felt anger, hate and self-pity most of my life and it led me to prison and hurting many people I loved. I wasn't going to allow my hatred to continue to do the same any longer. I continued to read and find scriptures that would help me get through this moment and the rest of the time here in prison. When I go to Ephesians, another one of Paul's writings, Paul says in chapter 4:

"Don't sin by letting anger control you? Don't let the sun go down while still angry. For anger gives a foothold to the devil."

He continues by saying:

"Let everything we do or say be helpful and encourage those around you."

I realized at this point what Tony was trying to tell me. I couldn't continue to live my life in hate and revenge and expect my life to change. I needed and wanted my life to change so that I could be the best soldier for the Lord and be the best man for Helen and the best dad for Sammy and Latisha. I must now accept the fact that Tony was dead and my actions could make things worse for me and my future. Frank was working on my parole hearing coming up so that meant I must not give the parole board any reason not to let me out of prison. The next week went by slow. I couldn't wait to see Helen and Latisha. I needed to hear her voice and tell me everything would be alright. I don't know how she has hung around so long through these times but I was glad she did. I don't know where I'd be without her. I would see the members that I knew killed Tony and they would give me a look like "I dare you." I was definitely up for the challenge but I didn't want that lifestyle anymore. So I would always keep walking, acting as if I'd never seen them before. The only question that really concerned me was what did Tony do to deserve to die? This was a question I wanted answered but would never be revealed. Finally, Sunday came and I was called to the visitation room. It was Helen and she looked beautiful. Latisha wasn't with her because she had come down with the flu. Helen and I talked awhile and I told her about Stacy and Sammy stopping by. Helen said she knew she received a call on Friday from Stacy. She said Stacy was a little hesitant at first. Stacy and Helen just watched the children play, not saying much to each other. Then she said Stacy warmed up to her and they began to talk about the past and the present, trying to connect all the dots. She said they had a good time and that the kids played well together and were very excited to meet each other. They decided to meet every week so that the kids could have time together whether they all stayed together or she and Helen got a break for a while. Helen also told me that the parole board hearing was in two months and Frank said he would be there to help represent me and get me prepared. That would mean I could get out of here before Latisha's next birthday if everything went well. My time was almost up so Helen and I gave each other hugs and kisses goodbye. She smelled so good and I didn't want to let her go. I eventually let her go then I remembered that I hadn't told her about Tony. She was sad that this happened and especially to someone that tried to do good things in a bad situation. I gave her one more kiss goodbye and she left. Over the next couple of months, each day seemed to drag. I talked to God a lot during these days to try to help me get through each moment and each thought of the things around me. I stayed away from the courtyard and kept to myself either having my nose in the Bible or working out in my cell. Pushups, sit-ups, and pull-ups became an everyday routine several times a day. I was probably in the best shape of my life physically, mentally and of course, spiritually. I didn't know what was ahead of me but I did know that I wanted God, Helen and the kids to be a part of it. I had felt empty most of my life always looking for something to fill this void that could never be filled. Now Tony had introduced me to God and this void was now being filled and every day I felt good and ready to move on, knowing that God would be there. No matter what lay ahead of me, I knew that I would be alright. Even if things got bad, it would be good and I would have the knowledge, strength and courage to push on and do the right things. Helen was always there every Sunday. This always gave me something to look forward to and to work toward. It helped pass the time knowing that Helen would be here in x amount of days. Each week, Latisha was growing bigger and talking better. It was unbelievable how much she was growing each week. The week before my parole board, Helen brought

Sammy with her. It was a great surprise having Helen and both kids. It gave me hope in knowing that I could fix my mistakes once I got out of prison and begin to build a better future. I knew it wouldn't be easy but I knew it could happen if I would keep the faith, be honest with myself and trust in God. I was also growing stronger and stronger in the Lord's word, studying and listening every day to become a better man. It was finally the day; the parole board was just in a few hours and I was sweating bullets. I was so nervous and excited to have the opportunity to at least have the chance to get out of prison. I knew that it was a long shot since I had only served around three years of my sentence but I was leaving that in God's hands. It was time and Frank and I were heading in. Over the next hour or so, they questioned me about how I felt, why I should be released and what I have done and will do to live a better life once I get out. I explained to them that I was at their mercy and I knew that. I explained to them about Tony, Helen, the kids, my plans and everything in between. I told them that if given the opportunity, I would make the most of my life and help to teach others not to fall into the same trap and lifestyle I did. The panel reviewed everything and taking all my thoughts into consideration, on March 28th of 2008, I was walking out of the prison and into the arms of Helen. It was so great to be free and before I got into the car I looked up to heaven and thanked God for allowing me another chance and forgiving me for all the things I had done. I got into the car and reached over and gave Helen a huge kiss and told her to get us out of there. There were certain requirements that I would have to fulfill over the next couple of years and I would have to report to my parole officer on a regular basis but I was free to play with my kids and be with Helen. At that point, I couldn't ask for anything more. I knew that I would also have to get a job and it would be tough considering I just got out of prison and had killed a man. My first thought was the pipeline but I wouldn't travel anymore because I wanted to be with my family. Also the state would not allow me to travel at this time. I called my previous boss and told him that I was out and looking for work. He told me to stop by and we would talk about the options and if they could use me under these circumstances. When I got to the office there were only a couple of cars. Most of the people must have left early for a long weekend. When I got into the office, Mary was at the front desk. She was surprised to see me but was grinning from ear to ear.

"It's good to see you again, Sam. How are you doing?"

"I am doing fine, Mary, and how are you?"

"I'm doing well," she said.

"I am here to see Robert about getting my job back but in a different capacity."

She released the door that separated the visitors from going directly to the back to the offices, and I headed back to Robert's office. When I got there Robert and Ed were waiting for me. They invited me in and told me to take a seat and they began to talk about my future.

"Ed and I have been talking and you are a very talented and a well-liked man in this industry, Sam. Every company we have sent you to had great remarks about you and your intelligence level about the industry was always one of the best. You worked very hard for us and we have decided to utilize your assets. We need someone to process data, analyze it and communicate with the customers. This would keep you in the office most of the time. Most of the processing even though in your hands can be done by your two technicians that we will give you. We are also going to put you in charge of all the local projects. This means start to finish. You are a good talker and that's what we need. We want to expand in these areas and we think that you are the man to head this up. You will have a support team and two engineers at your fingertips. You will be able to utilize whatever we have when it's available. This would mean a little travel within the state but no more than a few nights at the most. We are putting together a proposal for you as we speak. We believe you will be content with the offer."

At this point I was very happy and didn't know what to say. Obviously I was going to take the job; not only did I need it but it would be the perfect job for me. It was actually the best job I could have thought of. I had always respected both Robert and Ed and they must have respected me as well. I felt really good that this was happening — it felt right. I told them I would look over the proposal but that I was sure I would take the job.

"Go home, talk to Helen and come back on Monday," Robert said.

"Thank you both; I look forward to seeing you on Monday."

We all shook hands and I left. As I was walking out, I

told Mary to have a good weekend and that I would see her on Monday. She gave me a smile and said you too and I went to my truck. I was still working on getting my license so Helen was waiting for me outside. As I got in, Helen started asking me how it went. I began to tell her what was said and that I had to come back on Monday. You could tell that a ton of bricks had been lifted off my shoulders. Everything was coming together more than I could ever expect. God was taking care of things and it was a wonderful thing. My next step was to find a church that was right for me and the family, one that wouldn't judge us and allow us to love and worship the Lord. I knew that in some people's eyes I was still living in sin, and I was, but I needed time to correct this and do the proper things once everything was in order to do so. One example was the fact me and Helen weren't married yet, which had been on my mind but I needed a job first. I wanted to do things right and I was planning on how I was going to do that. That Sunday we decided to go to a church a couple of towns over. We had heard a lot about this church and every person I asked always brought up this church. So this would be our first church and first Sunday as a family to go to church. Stacy had brought over Sammy to stay the night, so all four of us were together. We were all pretty excited and a little bit worried. This was a new experience and a new lifestyle we were trying to live. We weren't sure what to do or what to expect. Neither one of us had ever been to church. As we walked into the church and through these two big double doors, we were greeted by a lady that had a smile from ear to ear and seemed so happy to see us. It felt really good but also our stomachs were turning from being nervous. We didn't know what time the service started and had actually showed up while one was in process. Luckily this church had three services to help with the growing pains of the church. The lady introduced herself as Kathy and said she would show us around and show us where the kids would go for bible study. She gave us a tour and along the way we dropped the kids off at their classrooms. At first the kids were a little reluctant but they went. After the tour we were invited to sit in on a class already in progress. At first we felt a little out of place since we didn't know anyone. The class was already half over so it wasn't long and we were to head down and get the kids. After we got the kids we headed to the chapel. Everyone was shaking hands and the music being played by the worship team was great. It was upbeat and modern and made us enjoy and feel wanted, and at this point we really didn't know anyone. We were really enjoying the atmosphere at this point and enjoyed worshipping in this environment. Two different pastors walked around and introduced themselves to us and encouraged us to continue to come back. After the worship team and prayer, the pastor got up on stage and began to speak. The kids were released to go to what they called junior church where they played games learning about scriptures and Jesus. The pastor began to speak and it was like he was talking to me. I had heard a lot about church and all the negativity around religion but this wasn't anything like that. It wasn't about traditions or politics. It was about Jesus and no other interference. It was as if Tony was there and led us to this church. The pastor reminded me so much of Tony; how he spoke, joked, preached and loved the Lord. We left there feeling great and knowing we would return. After church we headed to a local restaurant and grabbed some lunch and then headed to the park for the kids to play. As the kids played Helen and I talked about my future job, getting married, kids — everything. We had discussed some of these things through letters and small talk during visitation but it's not as permanent or real as now. We can actually put our plans into action. I was definitely excited about everything but I also wanted to do everything the correct way but that would be easy because the Lord would be directing our lives from now on.

CHAPTER 16

Helen and I were headed to the office Monday morning. I was a bit nervous and excited to see what would happen next. I would be getting my new license within the month and could get around by myself at least to work and back. We pulled into the parking lot and parked, and I looked at Helen and asking her for good luck. She straightened my tie and gave me a kiss. I jumped out of the car and headed to the door before I got to the door. I thanked God for the opportunity and I headed inside. Mary said "good morning" and released the door to come inside. As I walked around the corner, Mary told me they were waiting for me in the conference room. I walked into the conference room where six people were waiting for me. I knew most of them. Ed and Robert were both sitting up front. Charlie, the IT technician, and Dunn, an engineer, were both there as well. The two toward the back of the room I had never met but I had been gone a long time. Ed went around the room and introduced everyone and the other two were engineers, Mike and Jerry. Ed said Mike would be my right hand on the projects and any questions I might have concerning options or avenues I might need to take to sell the work. For the next three hours, we talked about what we needed, where we wanted to go, personal, and the future and present clients. Between us all we had a great discussion and there were a lot of great ideas. They had been really thinking about this and had brought a lot to the table, each one of us with a different perspective, and mine coming from the field of course. So I had a different view from the others and they all respected that and we used all our experiences to build a base for what we needed to do. After the meeting, Ed, Robert and I all went together to a local restaurant. We ordered our drinks and food and started talking about my pay and benefits. The deal was a great opportunity with most of my money being paid to me on my performance. I would receive a percentage of every contract sold, work received from data presentations, plus my base pay, medical, 401k and three weeks vacation to start. I was excited and surprised by the offer but didn't lead on to much. I had a big responsibility and would have to work hard. I was up for the challenge for myself and my family. I looked at them both and told them exactly that: I was up for the challenge and looked forward to being back to work with them both. When we got back to the office, I gave Helen a call to come get me. While I was waiting, I talked to several of the others I would be working with until Helen showed. I was going to get started Tuesday morning and I had a lot to do until then. Over the next two months, the job was going well. We had been pushing a few new ideas toward the clients and were sparking interest for some work. I had gotten my license back and was driving the truck again. It felt like old times except without all the old baggage. I had Sammy every other weekend and three days during the week. Both kids were doing great and we were adjusting well. The big night finally arrived and I had made special arrangements at a local fancy restaurant. I had bought Helen a ring and was going to ask her for her hand in marriage. I couldn't even think about being with anyone else. I loved her and I was ready to make things right. It was Friday and I had everything all planned out. I had ordered a limo and bought a dozen roses. I also had a red strapless dress laid out on the bed for her when she got home. I had picked up my tux at noon and the limo was going to pick me up from work at five. Helen was going to get home at around four so I called her shortly after that and told her to be ready at five-thirty and that her outfit was upstairs on the bed. She didn't understand what was going on but she played along and agreed.

"What about the kids?" she asked.

"Stacy will be over to pick them up for us for the night."

"Ok," she said and I hung up.

The limo showed up on time and everyone wished me good luck and a good time. I grabbed the roses and headed to the limo. When I got in he already had the wine display set and soft music playing. He was definitely trying to help me out and I appreciated it. I am sure he was working for a good tip. On the ride to the house, I had butterflies in my stomach and was so hoping everything was going to go as planned. We arrived at the house and I headed inside. When I got inside, I yelled for Helen and began to walk up the stairs. As soon as I got to the first step, she was standing at the top of the stairs. She was so beautiful the dress clung to her curves and it just sparkled. She was amazing. She made it down the stairs giving me a kiss and telling me how good I looked when I couldn't take my eyes off her.

"I figured it was time we had some fun so this is our night."

"Thank you. My dress is beautiful."

"You have no idea. You look so beautiful in it."

I had put the roses by the door so I reached for them and gave them to her. She took them with thanks and went to get a vase. She returned and we walked out the door. Her mouth dropped once again when she saw the limo. She gave me a smile and the rest of the way to the limo was a jog. As we climbed inside, she grabbed my hand and led me to the back seat. The limo driver hit the music on cue and we were on our way. I poured us both a glass of wine. I handed hers to her and lifted my glass to hers. I looked into her eyes and I told her how much I loved her and that I hoped she enjoyed this night. Once at the restaurant, we both stepped out as the driver held the door of the limo and then also opened the door to the restaurant. We headed in where they had a table all ready for us. The table was all decked out with flowers, candles and wine. You could see it in Helen's eyes how happy and excited she was.

After enjoying some wine, we ordered our food. I ordered a prime rib and a loaded baked potato and she ordered snow crab and lobster tail. As we were waiting, we talked about what we had been through and how our future would be much better. Then she started asking me if I wanted to have more kids. I hadn't been sure before but I think I would be alright with at least one more. I was enjoying Sammy and Latisha, and Helen had been teaching me a lot about being a parent. Once the food got there, we enjoyed the food and each other's conversations. We sat there a while and then I looked at her and grabbed for the ring in my pocket. I got the ring to my lap and began to tell Helen what she meant to me and that without her I'd be lost. Just as I was about to ask her, a lady walked up to our table. She immediately pulled a pistol.

"You killed my husband Jim and now justice will be served."

She pulled the trigger and a shot of pain went down my entire body. She shot me in the chest twice and walked away dropping the gun. She was tackled to the ground and the waiter called 911. I fell off my chair to the ground; the ring in the box fell out when I hit the floor. Helen came to the floor crying and yelling, telling me to hang on. Then she grabbed the ring and said, "Yes, Yes, Yes! I will marry you." Then she reached down and gave me a kiss. "You keep fighting, Sam, you have to. I am pregnant and your babies need a daddy."

I looked down and saw blood everywhere and figured it was my time to go. I didn't want to die but I was also alright with it too. I knew I was going to heaven and I began to pray and tell the Lord how sorry I was, how thankful I was and to watch over Helen, the kids and Jim's wife. The next thing I remembered was waking up in a hospital bed with Helen holding my hand fast asleep. I tried to move a little bit and Helen woke up.

"Hey sleepy head," she said.

"Hey, Babe. I love you. Are you really pregnant?"

"Yes," she said with a giggle.

You could tell see had been crying a lot and there were plenty of used tissues in the trash can and on the floor beside me. That night changed me forever. I realized a lot about my life and how I needed to live my life to the fullest and serve the lord the best I could. I saw how revenge was used to almost kill me and also destroy the life of multiple people because of one person's choices and the cost to all our families. I felt for Jim's wife and wish I could take back everything but I couldn't; I had to move on and I hoped that one day she would forgive me as well.

Helen and I got married as soon as I could stand up again. She didn't want to wait any longer and neither did I. We had everyone there and she looked so beautiful on that day; it was unbelievable. It took me awhile to get back to work and I was never quite the same after that. I lost most of the feeling in my left arm and I had a slight hitch due to one of the bullets injuring my spinal cord. The doctors originally predicted I wouldn't walk so I was happy to only have a slight hitch in my walk. I did eventually make it back to work and was more determined than ever. I had a lot of doctor bills and the twins were going to be coming any day. I began to work with my team to start building our company to be one of the best. We became the leaders in several fields and started becoming the company to hire to do the work in the field, which meant more money for the company and us. We became proud parents again of twin boys. Eventually we would have one more kid, giving us four together and Sammy.

CHAPTER 17

When I look back on my life, I realize how lucky I was and how blessed I am. I grew up with a terrible beginning and my life could have ended up anywhere, but the mercy of the Lord was upon me. I struggled and got into some trouble along the way but the most important things are how you end your life, not really how you begin it. You must learn not to forget your past but embrace it. Use the things in your life to help others so that they can learn and not make the same mistakes. Obviously life is hard and when abuse is added it's even harder, but do we give up and allow them to control our whole life or do we learn, grow, forgive and teach others? We are not alone. Many people have suffered from some form of abuse or neglect. Why allow others to control our emotions and lives?. Let's take back our lives and give it to the Lord so that the healing and growing may begin. Yes our lives will not become all peachy when we accept the

Lord and bad things probably will happen, but without the Lord it is much harder to go through. You need the strength, knowledge and the most important thing is the love of the Lord to face every day's battle. Why face a battle alone when you can have the Lord by your side? I destroyed a lot of lives in one way or another and caused a lot of hurt, but the Lord forgave me and has helped me to get back on track. The Lord can do the same for you! No matter where you are in life we must face the music of our troubles; you must forgive yourself and others like the Lord has for us. We must also begin to love one another as the Lord has us. God has set the example; we must just begin to follow.

There are many examples of the Lord's mercy in the Bible and how God continues to teach us that we must also have mercy as God does for each of us. You can't find a better example of God's mercy for us than the life and death of Jesus Christ and how he paid for our sins.

Here are a couple of other scriptures that give us other examples of how we should see and think of mercy.

When Jesus sat at Matthew's table and heard the Pharisees ask why he ate with tax collectors, Jesus said in Matthew 9:12–13. "Healthy people don't need a doctor — sick people do. Now go and learn the meaning of this Scripture: I want you to show Mercy, not offer sacrifices. For I have come to call not those who think they are righteous, but those who know they are sinners."

In this scripture, this tells me that those who believe in the Lord and are healthy in his word so seek those who are not healthy. We should not judge or carry on about them but we should try and help them whether or not we think they should be.

In Matthew 19: 22–35, Jesus said to Peter comparing a king and a servant and how mercy is given just as God gave us mercy we should also show mercy. In verse 33, Jesus said, "Shouldn't you have mercy on your fellow servant, just as I had mercy on you?"

In Lamentations 3:22, Jeremiah writes: "The faithful love of the lord never ends! His mercies never cease."

In these scriptures, God is talking of his mercy for us that he sent us his son to die for our sins and that if He can show such mercy why is it that we can't show some mercy for others? His love and mercy never ends for us so why should our love and mercy end? It all comes down to how we should act and love others who may not be at the place we are or maybe not even know the Lord at all. We should cram it down their throats or even preach but love them for what they are and where they are. That is showing the true message of the Lord.

ABOUT THE AUTHOR

My name is Michael John Rodgers Jr. I have been married for 10 years and have two beautiful children and one on the way. I am currently serving in the United States Army. While serving my country I also attend the University of Phoenix for a bachelor's degree in Organization and Security Management. My passion has always been to write a book and now my dream has come true. I will continue to publish books for adults as well as children's books.